Training or.

Training on a Shoestring

Getting the most from your time,
your budgets and your staff

KAYE THORNE AND ALEX MACHRAY

KOGAN
PAGE

First published in 1998

Kogan Page Limited
120 Pentonville Road
London N1 9JN

British Library Cataloguing in Publication Data

A CIP record for this book is available from the British Library

ISBN 0 7494 2573 3

Typeset by Northern Phototypesetting Co Ltd, Bolton
Printed and bound in Great Britain by
Biddles Ltd, Guildford and King's Lynn

For my father Kelvin Harris, my original inspiration, with love.

Kaye Thorne

To my wife Linda and children Ross and Ian whose understanding, enthusiasm and humour gave me the essential support and space to complete this book.

Alex Machray

Contents

Contents

Foreword

The shoestring principle is based on less equals more. In today's business environment everyone is tasked with making the right decisions, based on what is:

❑ Right for the business

❑ Right for the department/function

❑ Right for the individual.

Training cannot and should not remain in the domain of isolated Training and Development departments. Human Resource and Training professionals are faced with very real choices in determining what represents true value-added development.

The shoestring manager has to operate in a new environment, training has to be focused and organized. It is about demonstrating a maturity and sense of purpose. It is also about being resilient and looking after yourself so that you can withstand the challenges of working in a new way. Within this book we have focused on what we think it is essential for the shoestring manager to understand.

The shoestring manager needs to be able to distinguish between essential training and non-essential training. He also needs to fully understand and facilitate the process of change. Therefore the skill set/competencies of the shoestring manager are very different from the traditional manager of a training menu. The shoestring manager often operates within the following skill set:

❑ Aware of the 'big picture'

❑ Has an overview of T&D and learning solutions

❑ Excellent communication skills

- ❑ Able to influence, and has personal power base
- ❑ Highly organized
- ❑ Good interpersonal skills
- ❑ Able to facilitate
- ❑ Can act as an internal consultant
- ❑ Has good self-esteem
- ❑ Talks with assurance to team, senior managers and suppliers
- ❑ Benchmarks good practice
- ❑ Encourages others to proactively, continuously learn.

This book is about getting the most from your time, your budgets and your staff. We hope you find it useful.

Acknowledgements

In the development of this book we should like to thank the following:

❏ Tony Buzan for his innovative Mind Map method

❏ David A. Kolb for the inspiration behind How People Learn and his Experiential Learning Model.

❏ Peter Honey and Alan Mumford for the Learning Styles Questionnaire.

❏ We also acknowledge the work of those who created the models and concepts which underpin many T&D activities and to whom we cannot find specific references, eg SMART, Unconscious Competence, Urgent/ Important.

❏ Louise Thorne and Ross Machray for the design of the models and their technical hardware and software computer expertise.

❏ All the staff at the IPD Library for their very professional and responsive help in compiling the bibliography.

All authors need support and we owe a particular debt of gratitude to the following for their encouragement and interest:

❏ Chris Dunn and the whole TDA Team, David Mackey, John Murray, Paul Ewins, Chris George, Rob and Sue Ford, Bill Eldridge, Keith Harris, Paul Nicholson, Matthew Thorne, Joanne Crew, Doug and Lisa Twining, Kevin McGrath and all our other trainer colleagues. The Kilby family and staff at The Garrack Hotel, St Ives, Cornwall for continuing to provide an inspirational environment in which to write.

❑ Philip Mudd and the desk editing staff at Kogan Page for their innovative approach to publishing and for providing superb technical support and advice.

But, above all the very special clients and individual learners who ultimately have been our inspiration, and without whom this book would never have been written, our particular thanks to you.

Introduction

This book is designed to help people who find themselves with the responsibility for training within a changing environment.
You may be:

❑ A line manager with responsibility for training.

❑ A personnel manager with little or no experience of managing a training function.

❑ A Head Office practitioner with devolved responsibilities.

❑ A Further or Higher Education professional with responsibility for training.

❑ A small business owner, or partner in private practice.

Whatever your role, it is likely that a new perspective on training and development is needed. We have described this as Training on a Shoestring.

WHAT DO WE MEAN BY TRAINING ON A SHOESTRING ?

Training on a shoestring is our way of describing the situation prevalent in many organizations. It may be a result of one or several of the following factors:

❑ Your training budget is severely reduced as a result of cost-cutting.

❑ Organizational change has led to the training function being reduced in size or budget.

- ❏ Responsibility for training has been given to the business functions.
- ❏ Your organization is a small business, or professional practice with limited funds.
- ❏ You are a sole trader.
- ❏ You are an educational establishment.

Whatever your particular role or situation, the concept of training on a shoestring is about survival, or perhaps more importantly about survival with impact and influence.

As an individual within an organization you may have undergone major change. All the traditional approaches, and resources that surrounded you may have disappeared. You may find yourself in a situation where you have to make really tough decisions about what to fund and what to reject. You may be starting from a zero-base with no resources at all.

It is from within this context that the concept of the 'shoestring manager' has arrived.

SHOESTRING MANAGER PROFILE

The shoestring manager is resourceful, he uses every available route and contact to build his offering. He is not proud, he is creative, he uses his imagination to think outside the obvious. She networks brilliantly, she asks favours, she is selective and prudent.

Even if you still have a fairly healthy training and development budget, the suggestions that we make within this book can have the additional benefit of stretching your budget even further. Our approach can also help with the annual problem of demand exceeding the plan in certain months. It can also help to instil a discipline of planning, of monitoring costs, and of working in partnership with external suppliers.

We have used the generic term shoestring manager to denote the person who is managing the training on a shoestring; we recognize that you may have a number of job or role titles to reflect the different types of organisations that we have described at the start of this book. We have used 'he' and 'she' variously throughout to avoid gender bias.

HOW TO USE THIS BOOK

One of the key principles of this book is that although you may have a limited amount of time or resources it is important for you to find direct routes to the heart of training and development (T&D) needs, to think creatively about new ways of attracting funding and to adopt a shoestring approach to the management of T&D.

It is designed as a dip-in guide to enable you to read the section which is most relevant to you and your current situation. If you are completely new to training you may find it helpful to read the chapters in chronological order.

We have adopted an approach of highlighting and summarizing key concepts and principles within the text, and providing sources of further information in the Appendices. You may also be interested in our companion book *Everything You Ever Needed to Know About Training* which gives a broader overview of T&D.

THE 'BIGGER PICTURE'

The shoestring principle fits very well into the bigger picture of changes within corporate life in general. Many books have been written about the management of change or re-engineering, and there is a general acceptance within organizations of the need to do things differently. As part of this different way of doing things comes the realization that change touches every part of corporate organizations and academic institutions.

As part of this process training has undergone many changes in recent times; one of the most fundamental is the changing role of the training function. Traditionally training and development in large corporate organizations was often supported by a team of internal training staff, sometimes with a dual responsibility of training and personnel.

It was not unusual for there to be a hierarchy with a Head of Personnel and Training and a team of staff normally located at Head Office, with regional and area staff responsible for training and personnel in the field.

As organizations have been re-engineered and functions streamlined, responsibility for broad based training and personnel matters has often been given to line managers, with support from a much reduced central function. Equally the growth of small businesses has led to an explosion of smaller organiszations with diverse training needs.

Within this context there are a number of factors to consider; we have addressed them under the following headings:

NEW WAYS OF LEARNING

Recognizing the importance of understanding how people learn has become a key area of corporate development. We discuss this in more detail in Chapter 1. Why this knowledge is so significant to the shoestring manager is that by identifying how people learn it is possible to target far more effectively the resources within a restricted budget. In a more cash-rich environment it was possible to waste money on unfocused training, because if one method did not work then another route would be selected. With limited budgets the shoestring manager cannot afford to take that risk.

Helping people to understand how people learn means that you can target your solution more clearly to an individual. Any manager with responsibility for training should be able to use tools and techniques or commission someone to identify with their employees their learning style. Armed with this information, the individual should then be encouraged to identify and pursue their preferred route. It is unlikely that any one route will provide the solution, or in fact meet the exact requirements of their learning style, and so you should work to achieve the 'best fit' rather than an exact fit for the group. Wherever possible the training provision should still match the key principles of the preferred learning styles (as outlined in Chapter 1).

By providing a variety of training solutions you can develop people more in the 'round'. There will not be just one right way of doing things, and the outcome will be personal ownership of the responsibility to learn, supported by a sensible provision of resources.

NEW WAYS OF FUNDING

Many traditional sources of funding have now disappeared or been reduced. Therefore the shoestring manager has to think creatively and build different relationships to gain sponsorship for key projects. One way that this manifests itself is that funding for training which was once held centrally within a Head Office training function may now often be redistributed to business units.

An outcome of this is the realization that training can then be purchased externally or internally. In this context, internal training functions may find themselves being benchmarked against an external provider for quality of service as well as value for money. For internal providers to be able to survive they need to undergo a very careful review of their provision, and thereafter to introduce systems to ensure up-to-date provision and value for money.

The shoestring manager needs to explore the following options:

❑ gaining corporate support for particular initiatives

❑ liaising and networking with people with budgets

❑ externally recognizing where government funding may be available

❑ being selective and realistic about how they pursue this money

❑ reading any rules, or conditions and networking carefully to identify when grants and special opportunities are available.

We deal with this aspect in more detail in Chapter 2.

NEW WAYS OF THINKING

There have been some fundamental changes in the organization of training and development in recent years. In fast moving environments it is often critical to be able to recognize the business need and to respond appropriately. It is this need for business focus that has led to the devolving of responsibility for training and development to line managers. Many organizations believe that the closer you are to the sharp end of the business the easier it is to identify the real T&D needs.

While the identification may be easier, line managers are still faced with the issue of funding and delivering the solution, and this is when the traditional corporate T&D staff can find themselves with a change of role; some may continue to provide a brokering service to the business while others develop the skills of internal consultancy. Those that succeed do so because they recognize the level of change that is required, and they proactively move towards providing a new service.

Gone are the days when developing training solutions to meet a business need was like turning a supertanker. Try this today and by the time you are facing the right way the tide will have turned!

NEW WAYS OF MEASURING

Traditionally, T&D functions have been rather lax in the measurement of the effectiveness of training. There have been many reasons for this: too much focus on the design and delivery; lack of effective measurement tools, and lack of awareness of the need to link to business outcomes.

However, with reduced budgets it is even more important to measure the effectiveness of the training. It is now well recognized that at the start of any initiative the success criteria should be identified and the outcomes reviewed against this criteria. The closer that T&D matches the business needs the more accurate the measures can become and then the role of T&D becomes much more significant. Often funding will not be available until the success criteria have been agreed.

Having set the scene, the rest of this book is about putting it into practice and we hope you find it helpful.

You can contact us at The Inspiration Network, PO Box 125, Bristol BS15 3NF, England. We look forward to hearing from you!

Getting started

Having a great idea about training is not enough, you need to be able to translate that germ of a idea into reality. It will require some careful thought on what the training is designed to achieve, who the training is meant for, gaining support from others in your company, and how you will go about affording this event. All this may seem daunting, but if approached in a logical way there is no reason why you will not be successful.

But before we start looking at translating your idea it might be useful to say what we mean by a 'training on a shoestring' manager. The shoestring manager is someone who has been given responsibility and specific training task to perform; someone who has decided to improve performance with his or her workgroup, or it could be someone who is a specialist trainer or personnel officer who has to train staff within limited resources. In essence the training shoestring manager is someone who is attempting to improve performance with very little resources and is looking to get value for money.

THE SYSTEMATIC APPROACH TO TRAINING

It might be useful to describe from the outset a logical framework for training, sometimes called the systematic approach to training. The total training process can be regarded as a cycle and this is illustrated in Figure 1.

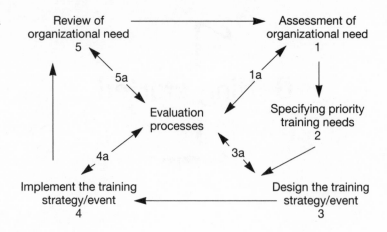

Figure 1 Training process cycle.

The following paragraphs give a quick overview of the cycle which is used and reflected in this book. As you will see later, where you start on this cycle can depend on your role and responsibility but to keep this simple we will start at step 1.

Step 1: assessment of organizational needs The aim of this step is to identify, agree and obtain support for the contribution that training and development can make to the organization's goals. This will include understanding organizational aspirations and the problems in reaching them, what training provision exists at present, identifying stakeholders and the level of their influence, and not least for the shoestring manager, the extent of any financial support. At the same time as this analysis is being conducted step 1a informs and develops evaluation criteria such as costs, desired outcomes, and judgements about value for money that will be used to define whether any training has been worthwhile.

Step 2: specifying priority training needs The aim of this second step is to identify training needs, to agree training priorities for staff and to assess and agree the resources required. This will involve agreeing with key stakeholders what needs to be addressed first, in order to meet the most pressing organizational requirements. Now is the time when the shoestring manager begins to tease out exactly what the training plan will deliver in terms of learning outcomes. Having clarified at the first step the training gap in global terms, this step articulates in more specific ways those related to a specific target audience. This clarification process will also include funding arrangements.

Step 3: design the training strategy/event   This step aims to design cost-effective training plans and strategies to assist staff to achieve learning objectives. This is the stage when having clarified broad outcomes we define individual learning objectives, and consider what training methods will best meet those needs. This could be a whole range of training events or just a single event. Objectives formulated at this phase will be linked to a evaluation strategy, step 3a, designed to measure expected outcomes both during and after the events.

Step 4: implement the training strategy/event   Step 4 aims to deliver the agreed training plans and strategies, to support learners, and to meet individual learning objectives. Through step 4a evaluation techniques are applied to check on individual learning as the course progresses to ensure that the chosen methods are working. As a result of the evaluation data, it may be necessary to adapt the training material to ensure the learning needs are met more cost-effectively.

Step 5: review of organizational needs   The aim of this final step is to review organizational needs in the light of the training. Although very similar to the first step in the way it is conducted, this step is looking to measure the effect of the training on the organization. Key questions about organization capacity and capability will need to be asked. The evaluation strategy, step 5a, will help determine to what extent desired training outcomes have been achieved in terms of both cost efficiency and cost effectiveness.

An essential issue for the shoestring manager is to define who does what. By using this systematic approach to training it is possible to articulate the boundaries of your responsibilities and your expectations of others involved in the process. You do not need to deal with every aspect of the cycle if that is someone else's responsibility. You may only be required to design and deliver the training, in which case steps 4 and 5 are of prime interest. However, someone else has to have considered the other steps otherwise you will have little chance to demonstrate that the training has been value for money – which is at the heart of being a shoestring manager.

GAINING AN OVERVIEW

Gaining a sense of the whole picture and how training fits into that picture is an important step which will help provide a sense of proportion. This is particularly important when it comes to selling your ideas to others who may not be so enthusiastic. There are a number of starting points in this process but perhaps a first one could be to ask why you picked up this book? There could be a number of reasons:

❑ you are not satisfied with your business's performance;

❑ you think that training might help raise morale;

❑ individuals' effectiveness is not what it could be;

❑ customer complaints are growing;

❑ you have a legal obligation to train staff, for example on Health and Safety matters;

❑ your competitors seem to have gained an edge or are getting closer to your markets;

❑ you consider training and development will be an aid to recruitment and retention of your staff;

❑ your staff need professional development and outside provision seems a bit expensive.

This is just a short list of the many reasons for considering that training could offer a solution to an organization's problem. We could go on for some time listing the possible reasons but at the heart of it is one fundamental question when considering training solutions,

'What's the problem?'

If you haven't got a problem you have to ask yourself why you need the training.

Perhaps first we need to be clear about what we mean by a problem. A working definition for a problem could be something that is difficult to deal with. This need not be something unpleasant as there are situations where something going well causes a problem, for instance where a firm has more orders than it can handle.

So, having started to answer the first question, the next is,

'When will this problem cease to be a problem?'

This allows us to establish the gap between the current situation and the desired position – your goal. Once established, you will be in a better position to judge whether a training solution is the most appropriate.

The following questions will start to help you establish your goal:

The outcome expected:

❑ Who will need to be involved in this result?

❑ What specifically will have happened when you reach the expected or desired outcome?

❑ When will this be, or need to be, achieved?

❑ Where will the result occur, (ie in all locations or just one)?

Success criteria – your measures for acceptability:

❑ What standards of quality do you expect will indicate your minimum level of acceptability?

❑ What quantity standards will you want as a minimum level of achievement?

Resource limitations:

❑ What are your limits or restrictions in terms of time and/or money?

❑ What resources in terms of people and/or equipment are required?

❑ What is critical now?

❑ What is essential in the future?

❑ What is urgent *and* important?

Now the goal should be summarized in one comprehensive and concise statement, then checked to make sure that it describes the outcome rather than a strategy. It is important not to confuse *ends* with *means* at this point. This statement will act as a reminder of what you are trying to achieve particularly when considering the solutions and avoiding the seduction of an answer which is not entirely focused on your problems. The statement will also be invaluable in gaining commitment from others, and we return to this later in the chapter.

Taking time to clarify your goals fully can help avoid limiting the possibilities in achieving them. Perhaps when drawing up your statement of goals you should be aware of some pitfalls:

❑ holding preconceived ideas about the *causes* of the problem;

❑ regarding the problems from only one standpoint – you need to avoid introducing your and any one else's bias in an area which could conceal a more balanced interdisciplinary view;

❑ ignoring how the problem is perceived in other parts of your organization;

❑ incomplete problem diagnosis – that's to say jumping for the easy or obvious answer rather than checking findings further;

❑ mistaking symptoms for problems by failing to differentiate between cause and the effect.

It is important to bear in mind that not all problems will necessarily be solved by training alone. For example, if the systems you use are inefficient there is little point in spending resources training people to operate an inefficient system; the first step in this case would be to address the systems issue first and then train your people. Through these opening chapters you need to keep an open mind, and to recognize that a training solution is not necessarily your first action.

The following categories include some of the problem areas that need to be considered before a training solution is applied. It may be that part of the solution to this problem is an educational process.

❑ *technological*: includes poor equipment; inadequate processes such as disorderly target setting;

❑ *environmental*: difficulties would include issues such as working conditions;

❑ *financial/planning*: includes payment structures; forecasting arrangements; financial and budgetary planning; the lack of monitoring and control systems;

❑ *structural*: organizational issues such as corporate objectives & the direction of the organization; the company hierarchy; management style;

❑ *communications*: information flows both formal and informal cultural barriers to change; performance reporting, the way that success or otherwise is fed up the line; inadequate personnel systems including performance appraisal arrangements; general ignorance of the organization's communication channels.

Other sorts of problems could be human. These include issues that can be successfully tackled by training, but others such as attitudes, conflicting values, or lack of motivation may demand more that just a training solution.

But let us assume that the matter you wish to address lends itself to training – where do you go from here?

ESTABLISHING THE EXTENT OF THE PROBLEM

Throughout this book we are attempting to obtain the best value for the money invested in your training. In convincing anyone to provide resources either in the shape of money, staff or equipment, it strengthens your case if the identification of the training needs is conducted systematically rather than as an *ad hoc* exercise.

Some companies engage in a major fact-finding exercise to analyse their training needs. These investigations can be at organization, operational, or individual level. But these all-encompassing projects are expensive and are often only undertaken when major change is required. However, some of the principles and techniques involved can still be employed by the shoestring manager. A popular approach is to continually assess the organization's needs using a dual process of top-down and bottom-up. Top-down is driven by the organizational business strategy, and the bottom-up process by staff and their line managers identifying individual needs.

Top-down might include factors such as:

❑ business performance;

❑ improved customer care;

❑ new legislation;

❑ recruitment and retention of staff.

Bottom-up could include:

❑ individuals' effectiveness;

❑ reducing accident rates;

❑ developing a flexible work force;

❑ using new equipment or technologies.

TRAINING AUDIT

Before designing new training solutions it is a good idea to discover what exactly is available in your organization. Although you may think at first glance that nothing exists, ask yourself how you currently inform staff about the tasks they have to complete. It would be very unusual for a new member of staff to come into the company and become fully effective straight away. So look for evidence of induction training and job training as a starting point. By asking questions such as:

❑ What do we do when new equipment arrives?

❑ How do we make sure Health and Safety issues are addressed?

❑ Do we ever take on work-experience students?

It is possible to build up a picture of the way training has been handled in the past.

Hopefully this detective hunt for clues and evidence will not be necessary, and your organization will have clearer examples of training activity.

Many companies have given training and development a higher priority in recent years as they came to realize that this is a fundamental part of managing the change to make the organization more effective. The scale of this training effort may vary, but an important feature is the desire to link training priorities and resources with strategic business needs. Training is regarded more as an investment that brings rewards than an overhead that has little or no bearing on organizational performance. Establishing this link in your organization should play an influential part in gaining commitment to your plans. Once the connection between the business plans and training is made, there is a greater likelihood that the resources will be made available to you.

A key feature of training on a shoestring is always looking to get something for next to nothing. Although it will be tempting to do your own thing, using the experiences of others and learning from their mistakes will go towards you achieving your goals at lower cost.

Another feature of the training audit should be to assess the levels of skills and knowledge that already exists within the organization. This is designed to establish exactly what talent you have got out there and how you might use it – think shoestring !

You could tackle this exercise by simply listing the things people are good at but this will not necessarily give you the answers you want. A more systematic approach focused on the demands of your training concept can provide a more reliable source of information particularly when it comes to targeting the training or getting people to help with the delivery of that training.

The first step is to list the skills, knowledge and attributes needed to successfully overcome the problem you have identified. Visualize the way you want it to be and ask yourself what will the staff be doing? What things will they *know*? How will they be *doing* the job? If you are stuck try using documents such as job descriptions and job adverts to give you a start. Talk to other people who may have a view or vested interest, such as line managers, users, customers and clients and ask for their input. List skills, knowledge and attributes down the left hand side, and across the top list the level of ability to create a Needs Identification list:

❑ needs training

❑ needs practice

❑ competent level one

❑ competent level two

❑ not applicable

❑ knows nothing

❑ knows a little

❑ knows enough to get by

❑ knows a fair bit

❑ knows the job well – enough to train others not relevant to job

❑ still learning the basics

❑ getting by

❑ needs development

❑ very familiar with the work

❑ great deal of skill and expertise.

You can then rate each employee against this list. This will provide you with information not only about those who might be able to help with the training but also provides a perspective on who else might benefit from the training you are planning. It is important you should also take feedback from the employees themselves.

IDENTIFYING THE AUDIENCE

The training audit only provides part of the picture as it focuses on a broad spectrum of skills, knowledge and attributes. Identifying the audience takes the process into greater depth. You can use the same matrix approach but this time the list on the left hand side will identify the detail points each member of staff needs to know or be able to practice in relation to the topic for training. You will have obtained this list from the Needs Identification you did earlier to identify exactly what the problems were. Across the top will be an assessment of how competent the member of staff is against each item. This will provide you with a perspective on the level of depth you will need in your training.

Another aspect of identifying the audience is how each individual learns best. It will be necessary when designing the training event to try and match the style of the training with the way that people take in new information most comfortably. For example, to ask members of staff who are used to practical applications to learn by reading a technical manual may not be the most effective method. Such people may prefer to learn by getting involved rather than dealing with the matter as an abstract. Others may wish to deliberate on a matter in order to come to understand the issues in their own way. Elsewhere in the book (Chapter 5) we explain more about learning styles.

Motivating staff to obtain the best from the training is a factor sometimes overlooked when putting a course or other training methods into place. It would not be unusual for each person to ask the question,

'What's in it for me?'

It may be about whether there is any reward either financial or otherwise. For others it could be about job security, and for some the chance of better job satisfaction could be the motivating factors. There are undoubtedly other reasons that drive staff to participate. For everyone the opportunity for personal development will be present. You will need to tap into that desire for development when designing the training.

It should not be surprising to encounter some staff who do not want to take part. Many of the reasons could be the negative side of those motivating factors identified above. Things such as being able to reward people for the acquisition of new knowledge or skills, or the perceived devaluing of their current work status or position. There will be some who consider that they do not need the training because they consider they already have the necessary qualities as part of their attributes. Your training audits will have given you a clue on this matter. The fact that someone already possesses a number of the qualities required should not necessarily prevent them from taking part. With the right presentational skills they could provide a valuable source of tutorial help to those less experienced. However, participation could be helpful for their own personal development.

In order to put this into context it is necessary to explain about the way we learn new skills. This process can be broken into four phases.

Phase 1: Initially we are at the stage of *unconscious incompetence;* that is to say unaware of the skill – ignorance is bliss !

Phase 2: We start to learn at the level of *conscious incompetence* when suddenly awareness of how poorly we do something shows how much needs to be learned.

Phase 3: By gaining some knowledge and with practice and experimentation we become *consciously competent.* We know how to do it right, but need to think and work hard to keep it going well.

Phase 4: Eventually, with frequent application, we arrive at a level of *unconscious competence*. It seems natural and easy and doesn't require so much concentration.

However, in order to maintain that level of unconscious competence we need from time to time to raise our level of awareness of just how competent we are in performing a particular skill; in the same way sports stars examine their performance to ensure no bad habits are creeping into their game.

This process also helps in understanding the problems people have in participating in learning events. Faced with the need to tackle new skills some may need to climb the skills development ladder again and this can be even more difficult when staff around them are already competent. Understanding this potential barrier to learning is an important part of helping staff come to terms with change.

4. Unconscious competence
(Integrated; natural)

3. Conscious competence
(Moving from being awkward to skilled)

2. Conscious incompetence
(Uncomfortable)

1. Unconscious incompetence
(Unaware)

GAINING COMMITMENT

Although you may be keen to undertake some form of training initiative, others in your organization may not have your enthusiasm. Gaining commitment is a key step in creating successful training.

So how do you go about getting that commitment?

The opinion of people both inside and associated with your organization all exert an influence on it. This will be true for your plans to introduce new training – a change. Very few individuals in an organization have sufficient clout to get things done unilaterally, they have to work with and influence others to bring about change. These individuals therefore tend to identify themselves with groups with similar aims, values and expectations. Identifying the individuals (stakeholders) and influential groups (stakeholder groups) who will be affected by your plans for change, and mapping their level of relative influence to help or hinder is vital in gaining commitment. This is called a stakeholder analysis.

Earlier in this chapter you identified the training audience, who are stakeholders and will form part of the stakeholder analysis. Conducting a stakeholder analysis is not difficult. You start by listing or brainstorming all the people connected with your organization. This will almost certainly include the staff and managers and will perhaps include shareholders, customers and directors. Each analysis will be different for each organization. It is worth remembering not to lean too heavily on the hierarchy of your organization as this may lead you to overlook groups lower down in the hierarchy who wield considerable influence in your project, for instance, securing the commitment of security guards in explaining building security to new entrants on an induction programme.

Having got your list you need to decide on the significance of these people in relation to your training project. For example, you may need clearance from your finance manager/director for resources or agreement from managers to spare their staff for the training. Remember that although some groups of people may not have a direct influence they may still like to be kept in touch with developments, so don't disregard them completely. You could organize this information in the form of a grid; an example is given in Appendix 1.

Gaining commitment to the training is no different from any other attempt to get people to change. With luck you will not encounter any resistance, but it is well not to assume everything will go without a hitch. In any business planning it would be naive to believe that the implementation of those plans would not be hindered by individuals who thought that their vested interest was being disrupted by those plans. Planning for training is no different. Whole books have been written about change, and we give a few of these in the reading list at the back, but the key to gaining commitment is proper planning.

Look at your list of stakeholders and ask yourself, 'What is likely to be their reaction to these plans and how can I get them on board?' The following four actions can help clarify what you need to do:

❑ Involve – commitment is more likely if people are party to the plans. Don't keep them in the dark until it is too late for them to contribute to the development process.

❑ Illuminate – people may be unaware of the problems facing the organization. The need for new techniques, knowledge or skills can often pass people by who are closely involved in the day-to-day process.

❑ Inspire – change and its consequences are a worry for some people. If someone has a level of expertise developed over a period of time they may feel their position threatened if they are asked to do something new. Reassure them.

❑ Implement – be prepared to be flexible in your approach to implementation. For some people, trying out new approaches in a step-by-step way is more reassuring and can assist the learning. Where resistance outweighs the pressure for the need for change you may even need to consider postponement.

During the phase of gaining commitment your communications skills need to be sharp and your listening skills even sharper! And having got your people on board, it doesn't end there as you will need to keep key players informed of how things are progressing, or not, as the case may be. More is said about this in Chapter 7.

TRAINING NEEDS ANALYSIS

The training needs analysis is an essential part of determining your training strategy and cannot be skipped. Having clarified the organizational goals and the required levels of performance to deliver those goals, the needs analysis seeks to determine the present level of performance. Any gap between desired and present levels of performance will help determine the target areas for training, and importantly for the shoestring manager, the priority order of that training.

The research techniques and sampling issues for conducting this analysis are exactly the same as those used when evaluating training, only the focus of the enquiry is different. During a needs analysis and evaluation you are attempting to measure the gap between existing and subsequent levels of performance. So techniques such as:

❑ observation

❑ tests/exams

❑ interviews

❑ questionnaires

❑ critical incident diaries

❑ repertory grid,

are all valid. Details of these and their relative ease of use is given in Chapter 7.

The interesting outcomes of the analysis for the shoestring manager is how the needs of various groups and individuals compare with the organizational outcomes expected by key stakeholders. The evidence for the learning objectives may be compelling but the shoestring manager will be looking to get best value from the training. Rating how important each need is in terms of the overall goals of the organization can be a demanding task. Some may be valid but not important. You will remember from earlier in this chapter that where resources are limited you need to be asking questions such as:

❑ What is critical now?

❑ What is essential in the future?

❑ What is urgent *and* important?

Using such guiding principles it is possible to list the training needs in priority order. Agreement of this order of priority is a process conducted with key players and not necessarily with all the stakeholders. It is important not to lose sight of what the original problem was considered to be.

Part of your overall training strategy has to ensure that the cost of conducting the training needs analysis is kept in proportion to the overall budget available for this training project which we discuss further in Chapter 2.

BUDGET ALLOCATION

A fundamental problem for the shoestring manager and a key assumption in this book, is the lack of resources to support training. We use the term 'resources' rather than money alone as this provides a wide interpretation of the means to support any training effort and could include:

❑ money;

❑ time;

❑ participants' salaries and expenses;

❑ trainers' salaries and expenses;

❑ accommodation including offices and perhaps training rooms;

❑ office equipment (computers, photocopiers, etc);

❑ training equipment (overhead projectors, flip charts, etc);

❑ stationery and other consumables;

❑ production and printing of training material.

It may be useful from the outset to establish whether your organization has any protocols or rules for obtaining resources, or indeed using the resources you already hold in a different way. Many a training project gets off to a shaky start because one or more influential stakeholders are offended by assumptions contrary to organizational policy. Using the list above it may be worth your while to list the likely resources that are available for 'free', what might be available in-house for some exchange in kind (such as places on the training event) and what will cost hard cash. You might find the proforma in Appendix 2 useful.

Whether you are given a budget to work within or are expected to estimate the costs before any resources are released, you need to have some idea of the broad cost parameters. This should be established during Step 1 when examining organization needs. You must have established the resources ground rules before you start the training needs analysis, as this phase has cost implication.

'How much will it cost?' is the dreaded question sometimes posed to the shoestring managers when first suggesting their ideas to a senior manager. Often in the early days it is difficult to give a ballpark figure. You are faced with the dilemma of giving your best guess which could run the risk of leaving you seriously under-resourced later on, or worse, the idea is killed off there and then. The lesson is to do your homework before even suggesting the notion of training. Unless you are coming up with a unique training problem the chances are that someone somewhere has done something very similar. All you have to do is to find how they tackled it. This will provide the ballpark figure you need.

Of course what someone else did for a similar problem may take the cost beyond your likely means but by using cost-effective analysis it is possible to assess what the various alternatives might cost. With this type of analysis we attempt to compare the relative costs of two or more training solutions that are intended to have the same or similar learning results to the ones you are seeking. Alternatively you could look at training events that cost the same and examine the relative outcomes. Wherever possible we compare like costs with like. A list of the costs you might take into account are listed in Appendix 2. Generally speaking it is probably more prudent to rely hard rather than soft data in your comparison. This is because in some organizations the soft data may have a different value. Professional Personnel and Training Associations such as the Institute of Personnel Development will often have data bases that can be interrogated for information on possible training solutions.

Once you have got a clearer idea of the training objectives it is easier to put a price on the cost of the training support. If your budget allows you to use external training solutions careful consideration needs to be given to the contract you award. A loosely worded contract will allow less competent consultants to deliver what they consider is required, which may not meet your expected outcomes. A contract needs to spell out clearly the outcomes you expect, together with a strategy to evaluate those outcomes. Just because this is an agreement with an outsider you should not forget the earlier mentioned discipline of summarizing your goals in one comprehensive and concise statement, checked to make sure that it describes the outcomes rather than a broad strategy. Avoid confusing *ends* with *means*. This is not to say that external training providers will purposely attempt to sell you short, but that any lack of precision may lead to misunderstandings; it is not much different from asking an architect to design and build a bridge, without any other specifications. You could end up with a construction from rope... to link up with a four-lane road!

Looking for solutions

Having undertaken your initial audit or needs analysis, how do you find the solution? The shoestring manager, as we discussed in Chapter 1, needs to adopt a very flexible approach to providing a solution.

It is important to establish an assortment of providers who can meet your needs. This can be achieved in a variety of ways:

❑ Identifying very clearly an overview of the needs.

❑ Prioritizing the demand.

❑ Exploring the range of potential solutions, 1–1 coaching, internal/external delivery, open/distance learning, multimedia.

❑ Match the providers and potential solutions to the individual and organizational need.

Further details on each of these solutions are provided in Chapters 4–6.

FUNDING

As we discussed in Chapter 1, training on a shoestring means making the best use of the money/resources available. It means that you make careful choices and prioritize. This prioritization still may mean the delivery of major training programmes, but is more likely to mean using different techniques to reinforce the learning. Investing in the development of coaching skills, facilitation skills or setting up a learning resource centre may involve a significant investment initially, but the benefits will be much more significant longterm than perhaps the delivery of just another series of training programmes.

The shoestring manager should always be thinking 'Where does this particular piece of training fit into the overall business picture? What benefits or linkages could this investment yield?' Equally he should be benchmarking and asking the question, 'Should I invest in this, is this the best value for money and a useful underpinning?'

How you manage the funds depends on your role and the organization in which you operate. As we highlighted in the introduction, there are a number of contexts for the shoestring manager. Depending on your context your approach to funding will vary enormously.

In a cash-rich environment money was often thrown at training without careful identification of training needs; large-scale programmes based on a 'sheep dip' approach often consumed a major part of the annual training budget. As a result of a reduction in funding and the increased understanding of different solutions to meeting the training need, training budgets are now much more focused. However, funding is still one of the major concerns of the shoestring manager, because this is the area which underpins so many other considerations.

The first step is to identify how your budgets are structured. This in itself may prove to be an interesting task, particularly in organizations that have undergone major change.

A budget allocation that was once given to the human resources or T&D function may now be divided up in a variety of ways, eg: some or all of it may have been devolved to the business functions on the basis that they will use it to purchase T&D and learning solutions from an internal T&D function or from external providers.

This model can operate on two assumptions: (1) Salaries and basic operating costs are covered in the corporate business plan. (2) The T&D function is a profit centre and has to cover its costs.

This level of commerciality can present a challenge to head office training functions that may have been previously protected from this aspect of the business. The converse is equally true in that it can also provide a tremendous sense of achievement when an internal function is benchmarked against an outside provider and wins the business.

There is of course a hard edge to this: someone, and it may well be the shoestring manager, has to be able to run the function on commercial lines.

If you are a sole trader or a small business/professional practice, your issue around finding funding may be very different. You may be working with a very limited budget where you have to justify to yourself or to other colleagues/business partners about the priority needs of the training.

You may also need to look externally for sponsorship and so the role of the shoestring manager is more of a 'resource investigator' to use a Belbin Team Role descriptor (see *Management Teams* by Meredith Belbin, Recommended Reading). In this context you may need to go to another function or outside the organization, to identify sources of funding or other resources. Often in this context you may be exploring the possibility of government money, for enterprise or small business start-up. Or you may be looking for support from professional associations in the form of bursaries, reductions in the cost of training, and provision of accredited trainers.

In education you may be looking for grants, special funding allowances, bursaries or other means of funding development.

Whichever route you follow, generating funding is a major issue for the shoestring manager. The principles of good budgetary control underpin everything in this book. When we work through each of the following chapters we are always aiming to identify the most cost-effective way of achieving your goals.

In the organizations where you have no budget at all, emphasis is on the importance of working in partnership with other parts of the business, and in developing relationships.

OPTIONS FOR MEETING THE NEED

The approach we suggest in this book is the need to look creatively at as many options as possible in the delivery of training (see Chapters 3–6). By adopting this philosophy some of the demands on the training budget can be greatly reduced.

As an example of this the shoestring manager could undertake the following:

❑ Identify the need;

❑ Explore the options;
  1–1 on the job training
  coaching 1-1 or team
  distance/open learning

27

internal training
open programme
facilitated session
secondment

❑ Supported by follow-up coaching and mentoring.

These are explored in more detail in Chapters 4–6.

ESSENTIAL DEVELOPMENT

The principles behind training on a shoestring ensure that when it comes to T&D you focus on specific areas. To illustrate the point we use a model that is often used in Time Management.

Urgent and Important	Important but not Urgent
Urgent but not Important	Not Important Not Urgent

Figure 2 Timescale model.

By focusing on key areas you should be able to identify the timescale for delivery in the following ways:

Urgent and important: these are critical training and development needs that arise because of changes within the business, or incidents that may have occurred, for example health and safety issues. Also problems which affect the viability of core business functions, products or services, will fit into this category.

Important but not urgent: this will identify those areas which need attention and forming into a plan, but do not require an immediate response, for example:

❑ preparing employees for a new piece of legislation

❑ the future launch of new products and services

❑ developing people for a change in role, or new responsibilities, or new ways of working

28

❑ a downward trend in key performance areas

❑ ongoing personal or organizational development.

These first two categories should form the basis of your ongoing training and development plan.

The remaining two areas are less critical, for example:

Urgent but not important: this may be something that is being driven by someone else, for example:

❑ A business planning decision is required for another part of the organization and may impact on the shoestring manager.

❑ An external supplier may be trying to persuade you to send someone on a course which they are running in the next few weeks. You can see that it could be relevant for one or two people, but it is not a high priority for you.

Not urgent, not important: an individual employee might wish to develop skills in an area completely unrelated to their position. They may be putting you under pressure to fund them. This would not normally be funded unless relevant to business goals.

Anything which has no relevance to your business really should not be featuring in your plan.

Using this model will help you to focus and identify where to channel both your energies and resources. We will leave you to consider just where the managing director's demand for time management fits into this framework!

Assuming you adopted this policy at the start of your financial year, you could plan your training and development as follows.

The realities around this model are that there will always be new 'urgent and important' coming into the plan, and consequently the percentage in this will always be high. There will also be seasonal adjustments, which will vary depending on your sector as training is an all year round process, though in some businesses operational demands mean that it is impossible to train people during some periods. In this case the budget will have to be phased and managed to meet these demands.

Some major initiatives require a cascade process where there is intense activity at the beginning followed by a phased reduction of involvement as it works through the business. This may mean paying external providers to design the programme and to train the internal team, followed by a reduction in cost as it is run internally.

The 'important but not urgent' sections form the basis of

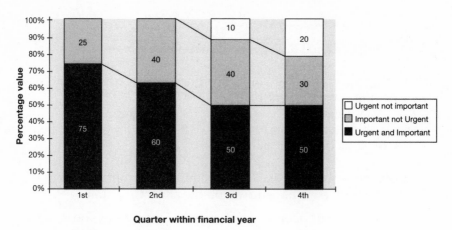

Figure 3 Scheduling T&D priorities.

ongoing development, of things that must happen, often on a regular basis. This may be technical training or training required to
meet legislative needs, eg IT training around the introduction of a
new software programme, or Health and Safety training.

The 'urgent but not important' sections may be agreeing with an
individual that in six months time you may be able to fund part of
their own career development programme, maybe an external
course such as an MSc or other higher qualification. In personal
terms it may be urgent to the individual, but you have to balance
these personal one-off requests with the broader picture of organizational development.

Special note

This does not mean not being supportive to personal development
is being realistic in terms of where you allocate your limited
resources. You do not withdraw your personal support; instead,
you work with that individual to identify alternative sources of
funding and/or training solutions.

Making it happen

MATCHING THE SOLUTION TO THE NEED

In earlier chapters we have highlighted how to identify training needs and how people learn (see Chapter 1), and how to prioritize training (see Chapter 2). With this knowledge it is then important to identify how to make it all happen.

We have already highlighted that as a shoestring manager you may be operating in a variety of situations, and so your interpretation of making it happen will vary.

If you are a line manager you may be required to deliver some training to your team, and this is likely to be either through on-job training, coaching, mentoring or some kind of personal development activity. Therefore we would suggest that areas of interest for you could be as follows:

❏ how people learn/learning styles

❏ coaching

❏ giving feedback,

all set within a working environment. There are other elements that can be useful to understand, but with limited time you may wish to focus on these first.

If you are a manager of a training function with greatly reduced numbers of staff you may be interested in the following:

❏ thinking strategically

❏ networking

31

❑ engaging external consultants

❑ evaluation.

As a partner in a professional practice:

❑ developing people

❑ using a learning centre

❑ coaching

❑ continuous professional development.

Overall as a shoestring manager you should not be expected to do everything, because you are working within a limited budget. Instead, you should have the role of a co-ordinator which enables the organization to benefit from your research and guidance, and your resourcefulness in identifying solutions.

Therefore we have assumed that you do not need an in-depth understanding of training and development. Neither do we expect that you would need to be able to deliver major programmes, or to design open/distance learning or multimedia materials. What is important however, is understanding the underpinning principles of all of these things so that you can purchase or commission wisely.

THINKING STRATEGICALLY

It is important to be able to think strategically; you will use this in a variety of ways:

❑ *Initially* for your own personal understanding of how the business runs.

❑ *Subsequently* in your work with your clients.

❑ *Finally* in managing your own pattern of working.

As the shoestring manager works in a variety of contexts we have taken an overview of strategic thinking here, and when we refer to clients these may be internal or external depending on your role.

Strategic responses are ones designed to build the 'big picture'. Thinking strategically means planning for the future, and thinking beyond the immediate and is far-reaching. Areas of consideration can be as follows:

❑ analysis of the current market place

❑ analysis of the competition

❑ looking at benchmark data (who else is doing what – comparisons between different organizations)

❑ projections for the future, again based on research and data available

❑ business planning, plans for expansion

❑ environmental factors or legislation

❑ risk assessment.

Tactical thinking is more immediate and responds to current situations.The responses generated in tactical situations tend to be opportunistic, and respond to the situations that may have arisen because of a shift in the market place, the actions of a competitor, or an opportunity/ threat which unexpectedly presents itself.

A shoestring manager working with an internal client often finds himself having to respond tactically while wishing to position himself as a strategic partner.

By aligning herself with her client the shoestring manager begins to build the basis of a more effective partnership in the future.

Actions that can be undertaken to think strategically are as follows:

1. Develop a 'business' awareness – read the business pages to gain a sense of current trends and issues.

2. Focus on specific parts of the business, either those you are currently working with, or those you would like to work with. Gather press cuttings and city/financial information about these targets.

3. Build a picture of your client – establish what issues might be on their mind. Where are their successes? What are their issues? What are their opportunities?

4. Think about the sector. Read the trade press. What are the competitors doing?

5. The closer you move towards understanding the business the

better you will understand your client. With experience you will come to understand their strategic thinking and eventually you will reach a position where you will be able to identify strategic actions with them.

6. In partnership arrangements this often means that you and the client will plan for the future together, putting together more considered training plans. The tactical responses will still remain, but these can be positioned within the overall strategic focus.

DEVELOPING A TRAINING STRATEGY

Should the shoestring manager have a training strategy? Some might say what is the point? Things change so rapidly that as soon as the ink was dry, priorities would shift and change, and who has time to write one anyway?

In reality the shoestring manager should have an overall training strategy, and as we have just discussed in the section on strategic thinking, one way that the shoestring manager can illustrate that they think strategically is to draw up their own strategy, built around the business strategy. It also gives a sensible reason for meeting with senior management, initially to identify the overall strategy and then to present your own training strategy.

It is important to set the overall parameters for the delivery of learning solutions.Under the overall umbrella of aims and objectives you can build in enough flexibility to meet the ongoing needs. By adopting this approach you will find it much easier to explain the rationale for the prioritization of training that you identify.

BUILDING RELATIONSHIPS

For the shoestring manager it is important to think very carefully about your time and use of resources. As a purchaser of training and learning solutions you play a very important role. This role is based on developing relationships with a number of key players:

❑ the decision makers or budget holders

❑ the sponsors of the training

❑ the learners themselves

❑ your current suppliers and potential suppliers.

Your role is to develop relationships with each of these key groups. To help you achieve this it is important to identify what each group expects.

The decision makers, or budget holders

This group, which normally includes senior management, will expect you to manage the budget effectively. This will include not exceeding the allocated amount, projecting budgetary needs in the future, and to keep accurate and up-to-date records on your spending. They will also expect you to manage suppliers appropriately and to provide regular reporting on the activities that you are undertaking.

The sponsors of the training

These are normally line mangers who will expect you to deliver a training or learning solution which meets their needs, delivered when they want it, and to a high standard within a set budget.

The learners

These will expect a training or learning solution which is stimulating, which matches their learning style, engages their interest, and meets their individual needs.

Your current suppliers and potential suppliers

These will expect a clear decision-making process, prompt payment, and a clear identification of what your organization and the individual learners require.

MANAGING THE PROCESS

Against this background, where do you focus your attention? In reality you have to manage the whole process. What is important however is to recognize how to prioritize your time and how to manage the limited resources.

One of the first instincts can be to try and do everything yourself. If you have training knowledge or experience you may feel that you can save money by doing the delivery yourself. However, as we discussed in the introduction your role should be more as a co-ordinator ensuring that the resources are managed effectively. In Chapter 1 we outlined a systematic approach to training.

Within this chapter we develop this approach to describe how to work in partnership to identify a learning solution.

Commissioning a solution

In identifying the right supplier it is important that you understand the likely process to be involved. Normally the cycle looks like this:

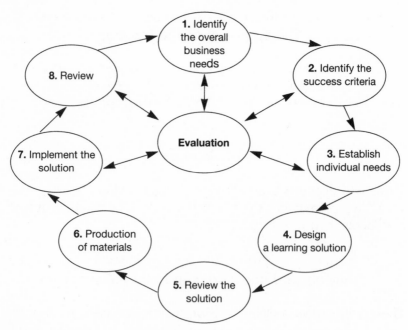

Figure 4 Sample consultancy process.

Therefore an external supplier will base their proposal on their involvement in each stage. However the experienced shoestring manager can use their own expertise to support the process. If we look at each stage in turn.

1. Identify the overall business needs: The shoestring manager can undertake this activity, normally this involves meeting with senior management, or line management, depending on the overall strategic relevance of the training. Questions that can be asked are as follows:

1. What business objectives are you trying to achieve?

2. What training needs have you identified? What new skills/ competencies are required?

3. From this list what is your priority order?

4. Are there any individuals who may need particular support?

5. At the end of this training what would you like people/or an individual to do that they cannot do now, or what would you like to be different?

6. If this training works, how will you measure its success?

7. How can this training help in the achievement of your business objectives?

8. Realistically, how much time can the individuals spend away from the workplace undertaking this training?

2. Identify the success criteria: By tailoring the above questions to include business objectives and success criteria you can identify the answers to Stage 2 at the same time. As we discuss in Chapters 1 and 7, the criteria for evaluation should be set up at the start of any project; for example the measurement of the following:

❑ the value of training to the organization,

❑ the involvement of line managers in the training process and the provision of information on the effectiveness of training design and delivery,

❑ costs, desired outcomes and judgements about value for money.

3. Establish individual needs: Once you have gained an overview you need to question a sample of the potential participants to identify their needs. Again, a representative sample can be identified with senior management during the initial interview. During these interviews it will be important to establish what previous training they have undertaken. Identify their current role, and what they would like to be able to do at the end of the training. As a result of stages 1–3 you should be in a position of writing down aims and objectives.

The aim describes the overall outcome of the programme, eg *To develop coaching skills in first line managers*. The objectives are something that participants are able to do at the end of the programme. Objectives should be SMART:

Specific

Measurable

Achievable

Realistic

Timed

When you are discussing your training needs with a supplier, you may give them the overall outcome and ask them to identify the proposed objectives that will be met as a result of the training. Their ability to write SMART objectives can be used as part of your selection process. Using the above as an example you should be looking for words like: describe, demonstrate, carry out, develop.

At the end of the programme participants will be able to:

❑ describe the way people learn,

❑ demonstrate effective skills of communication,

❑ carry out a coaching activity,

❑ develop action plans for putting the skills into practice.

Having identified the overall aim and objectives you are then in a position to work with suppliers to find a suitable solution.

4. Design a learning solution: One of the first questions to ask at this early stage is the type of solution required. It is easy to make the assumption, often endorsed by functional management, that a training course is the right solution. We explore other options in Chapters 5 and 6 where we examine in more detail other alternatives to training courses.

However, if you decide that a training programme is the correct course of action you need to consider how it will be provided. Usually there are one or two options: either use one of your internal training team (if you have such a team), or commission an external training consultant to undertake the design for you. An alternative option is to send your participants on an open programme. In making your decision a number of factors need to be considered:

❑ Availability of an internal training team. You may not have an internal team, or they may not be available to undertake your training. In some cases you may need to commission an external training consultant because of the specialist nature of the training required.

❑ It may be possible to discuss your organization's particular needs with the trainers running the open programme. Ideally, try to talk to the trainers themselves rather than the administrators, as this will give you the opportunity to make an assessment of their expertise. Without discussing the particular needs of individual participants you may be able to discuss the overall process involved.

❑ If you have a few people needing training, an open programme can be the best solution. However you need to look very carefully at the economies of scale. Often the same training providers will run an in-house programme for a fee which may be less than the daily delegate rate. The advantage of the internal programme is that it can be tailored to your specific needs. Always find out this information before committing to an external programme.

Whichever route you choose you need to be assured that the following key stages have been undertaken:

1. The overall aims and objectives have been identified.

2. The needs of different learning styles have been taken into consideration in the design of the programme.

3. A range of activities, exercises and different learning techniques have been incorporated into the programme.

4. The programme is timetabled to achieve the overall aim and objectives.

5. The pace and style of the trainers is appropriate.

6. An evaluation process is included.

5. Review the solution: Assuming you have commissioned a tailored programme, it is important to review the outline programme prior to the production of materials or delivery of the programme. At this stage, review the overall aims and objectives, and identify whether the proposed programme will meet the needs. Ask the training providers to talk you through the programme.

If it is to be a major organization-wide programme, you may wish to run a pilot programme with a representative group. This will give you the opportunity to test out the training delivery and the appropriateness of the material before going live.

6. Production of Materials: Here is another opportunity for the shoestring manager to review costs. Even if the programme is being run by external training you may wish to produce the materials in-house if you have the facilities, or you may have a preferred supplier of materials. You do not normally have this option on an open programme. This is something which is particularly important to establish at the start of the process before costs are incurred.

Even if the materials are produced by the training providers it is important to review the quality of the materials. Will you want full-colour or two-colour printing? Wire-bound or a binder? It is important not to produce materials which undermine the professionalism of the rest of the process and thereby the effectiveness of the learning processes. In this case we are talking about tutor guides or participant guides. We discuss the production of other types of material in Chapters 4 and 5.

7. Implement the solution: In the implementation of the programme there are a number of ways in which you can review the costs. You need to look carefully at the ratio of participants to trainer. If you have internal trainers it may be possible to match one of them with an external trainer, as in this way you are developing the skills of the internal trainer through train-the-trainer.

In some major strategic programmes external consultants are used for the initial set-up stage of the programme, followed by train-the-trainer and delivery by internal staff. In this way you can develop the skills of your internal team. You may also be able to negotiate a discount based on the delivery of a number of programmes.

Importantly, you also need to work with the line managers in the business to ensure that participants who are booked on a programme actually turn up for the event. In today's busy working environment participants can often find a reason for not attending a training programme without realizing the impact this may have either on cancellation fees, or the need to run additional programmes. This links back to Chapter 1 and our points about gaining commitment.

8. Review and evaluate: Whether the participants undertake training on an open programme or as part of an internal initiative, it is important to review the training. This needs to be undertaken at a number of levels:

The learners: ask the participants the following questions:

1. Did the training meet their individual needs?

2. Was it relevant?

3. Do they now feel more confident and competent as a result of it?

4. Should anything be done differently next time?

These reviews are normally carried out at the end of the programme. Feedback from the learners can then be fed back into their own personal development plans.

The line managers: review the outcomes with the participant's line manager – as a result of this training is this individual/or these individuals demonstrating new skills/competencies?

This review is normally carried out 3–6 months after the training is completed.

Senior management: overall review with senior management depending on the scale and scope of training: did this training intervention work?

This would normally be carried out at the end of training or as part of a significant training review. One of the outcomes of reduced resources is that you may find yourself with more accountability, and you might be asked to meet with senior management more often.

The trainers: ask the trainers to review with you the feedback from the groups above. Ask them to carry out their own evaluation of their performance. Did they meet their objectives and the success and evaluation criteria that they set at Stage 2? Would they do anything differently next time?

We discussed evaluation in Chapter 1 and we cover this in more detail in Chapter 7.

Evaluation and review are particularly significant for the shoestring manager as a way of ensuring that you are making best use of limited resources, but it also highlights any potential issues quickly.

From the eight key stages that we highlighted in Figure 4, you can see that it is possible to follow a number of approaches to providing a learning solution, and that the shoestring manager can, through their involvement, have considerable control over their training budget.

Every professional external training consultant should recognize the importance of skill transfer to an internal purchaser of training and should be prepared to work in partnership with you, involving you in the different stages of the process. They should also recognize the limitations of your budget and be prepared to work with you to identify the best use of your joint skills.

Shoestring checklist

✓ Gain commitment from the business.

✓ Work in partnership with other individuals and teams.

✓ Use influencing and negotiating skills.

✓ Set clear deadlines.

✓ Have contingency plans.

✓ Make effective decisions.

✓ Be aware of the 'big picture'.

✓ Work towards specific outcomes.

Tools and techniques

One of the outcomes of the changing role of the training function, and one of the challenges facing the shoestring manager is where to devote your energies. Depending on your role within your organization the concept of training on a shoestring will have a very different application. One common feature, however, across all roles and all organizations, is the shift from pure training delivery to thinking more strategically (see Chapter 3). The result of this is that the shoestring trainer/manager will have a very different focus when commissioning the delivery of training courses.

A traditional trainer may have turned up at an organization and delivered a training course on Time Management for example, and after encouraging the participants to fill out an evaluation sheet, considered his task complete. Providing he charged a reasonable fee and the training was well received and the participants fed back positive comments to their line managers, then this trainer could deliver the same programme on a fairly regular basis and the client would be satisfied.

In today's business environment and as a shoestring manager, you will be performing a number of roles, and it is critically important that you focus on the important aspects of training, ie the areas that will make a significant difference to the business. To be able to identify the critical areas you need to be able to align yourself with the business objectives.

Therefore when you are commissioning training you would need to follow the eight-stage process that we outlined in Chapter 3, and the prioritization process described in Chapter 2, and so it is unlikely that you would be commissioning training in the traditional way. A specific programme such as Time Management could only be justified if it led to the overall achievement of the business objectives. Although it may seem a harsh example and an insult to all Time-Management trainers it serves to illustrate an important shift away from what organizations have suffered from in the past, ie a menu of training programmes issued to the business which managers use without too much consideration.

When you are training on a shoestring you have to be much more selective and focused in offering a training provision, and as we shall illustrate in the next few chapters, the solution may not involve traditional training methods at all. There is also no rule that says training has to last for several days, in fact there is much to recommend short focused two-hour sessions, particularly if they are offered over a period of time such as an ongoing coaching programme, or series of masterclasses.

So in the shoestring climate, what does a shoestring manager/trainer need to know about training? As we have discussed elsewhere this really will depend on your role and your organization, but the rest of this chapter and Chapters 5 and 6 outline frameworks of some of the key techniques and processes that the shoestring manager needs to understand and on some occasions practise. This information can be supported by a number of other publications which we have referenced in the recommended reading list at the end of the book.

THE SHOESTRING SKILL SET

The techniques and processes that we illustrate below are built on the development of a particular set of skills which can be broadly described as follows:

❏ effective communication

❏ listening

❏ questioning

❏ observing

❏ giving feedback

❏ self-confidence

❏ creativity.

You will be required to demonstrate an enhanced understanding of all of these, plus the ability to manage the ongoing process of providing learning solutions. You might also want to refer back to the foreword to see the additional areas we highlighted there.

TRAIN THE TRAINER

We have already mentioned the importance of not getting too involved in the delivery of training. But depending on your role there may be occasions when either you or one of your team need to undertake Train-the-Trainer training. Basically, Train-the-Trainer training takes two main forms.

You attend a generic Train-the-Trainer training programme to help you prepare to be a trainer. If this is the case, use a reputable organization, make sure that there are plenty of practical sessions; initially with the form of medium that you would normally use and then with equipment that you might be required to use in the future. Ensure you practise using as many different media as possible such as overhead projectors, 35mm slides, personal computers and other audio-visual techniques. Ensure that you receive 1-1 feedback and ideally are videoed when you are presenting.

Increasingly, PC-based packages are being used by both small businesses and larger organizations for presentations. But learning how to effectively structure training to meet the needs of the learner is still a requirement for many organizations, and you may find yourself having to organize basic presentational techniques courses.Therefore it is important that whatever form of Train-the-Training you undertake it can also help you with the realities of your everyday situation.

A typical presentation skills course might include:

❑ presentational techniques,

❑ clarification of training aims and objectives,

❑ structuring presentations,

❑ selecting and using visual aids,

❑ handling questions,

❑ transferring learning to the workplace.

More specialist trainer programmes may include:

❑ a systematic approach to training,

❑ how adults learn,

❑ training strategies,

❑ identifying needs,

❑ interpersonal skills,

❑ designing training programmes,

❑ training delivery,

❑ evaluation design.

Alternatively, you may be invited as an organizational representative to take part in an internal cascade where you are trained to deliver a particular process or programme. Again, depending on your own personal level of expertise, ensure that you gain as much advice as possible from the trainers delivering the training. Ask for feedback and do not attempt to deliver the programme until you feel totally comfortable in doing so.

This is particularly important if you are new to training and you need to maintain your credibility within your organization. You may prefer to adopt a support role for a few events until you feel confident to undertake the major role. Always think carefully and review your workload before becoming involved in this activity because of the issues we have highlighted earlier. It is very easy to be enticed into delivering an exciting programme only to find that operational difficulties arise because you have stretched your time and resources too thinly.

COACHING

Coaching has a major role to play in today's organizations. The responsibility for coaching normally lies with someone's line manager. The shoestring manager may need to introduce coaching into the organization as a way of reinforcing learning, but also as a more cost-effective way of developing skills, knowledge, behaviours or attitudes.

Increasingly, organizations are recognizing the potential of coaching as a very focused way of developing their people. But for coaching to work effectively people need to be trained to coach. The scale and scope of this may be an important investment, but one which will have far-reaching implications for the future success of the organization. The development of a coaching environment can provide ongoing support to the implementation of all future training initiatives, as well as the development of on-job skills and competencies.

Where should you start?

Importantly the shoestring manager should identify the target group and follow the eight-stage process highlighted in Chapter 3. As part of this process you should ensure that everyone understands the significance for the organization of introducing coaching. Broadly this can mean:

❑ Adopting and selling at senior management level an overall coaching culture. This is critical for success.

❑ Line managers will need to be trained in how people learn and how to coach.

❑ Identification of needs, delivery of training and of giving feedback, within the context of 1–1 line management.

❑ Formal training, followed up by 1–1 coaching support by the line management.

❑ Everyone will develop enhanced communication skills: observation, questioning, listening, giving feedback.

❑ Line managers give time to be able to devote uninterrupted attention to the learner in order to develop new skills.

The payback from this initial investment can be enormous. An organization can really move forward as a result of adopting this approach.

In some cases it can dramatically reduce reliance on training courses.

The coaching process

Training people to coach may well be one of the areas that you decide to devote part of your training budget to, or you encourage the functions/ partners to purchase. As we discussed above, the overall benefit to the business of adopting a coaching culture will be much greater than just the initial training of people to coach.

Following the training you should expect people involved in coaching to follow the guidelines below.

A good coach will:

❑ Naturally demonstrate coaching behaviours in his everyday pattern of working.

❑ Encourage the development of specific skills and find a time and place to devote uninterrupted attention to the learner.

❑ Give praise whenever possible.

❑ Use questioning and listening skills to help the learner identify problem situations and the new requirement for skills, knowledge and behaviours.

❑ Be aware of body language and any other signs that demonstrate that the learner is having difficulties with the coaching; be prepared to try a different approach.

❑ Clarify the points discussed and, when appropriate, note the agreed plans of action.

❑ Ensure that coaching is a continuous activity.

❑ Recognize when further formal training is required in addition to the coaching.

❑ Reinforce the lessons learned from the training into the ongoing coaching.

THE SHOESTRING MANAGER AS AN INTERNAL CONSULTANT

Depending on your role, you may already be acting as an internal consultant. It may not be defined as such, but the services that you provide to the organization may follow a consultancy model, for example like the eight-stage process that we illustrated in Chapter 3. This process can be used by either an external training consultant or an internal consultant.

One area of development is moving away from the traditional role as a manager, a trainer provider or co-ordinator of training, towards the role of an internal consultant, and although you may need to invest in being trained in consultancy skills, this like coaching skills is a valuable long-term investment.

By developing a more consultative approach the shoestring manager can develop a more significant and accepted role in the organization. The organization will benefit through the provision of the following:

❑ A business partner who understands the 'bigger picture'.

❑ Who has an enhanced skill set and can contribute to the development of the business strategy, who can facilitate the decision-making process, and can help with team building and problem solving.

❑ Who will be able to identify the core training needs and who will recognize the urgent and important business issues and thus provide a quicker and more focused response.

❑ Who will demonstrate a high concern for evaluation and the setting of success criteria and who will react with a speed of response to required changes in training and development programmes.

❑ And lastly through the provision of highly flexible and tailored solutions to training and development needs.

The consultancy process

We have illustrated an eight-stage process which is based on working with a client to identify their training needs, but it is a process which could be applied to any consultancy intervention. A consultant would base their analysis on a number of key questions:

Understanding the relationship
Who is the client?
What is the brief?
What could be obstacles to progress?

Managing the relationship
Who are the key players?
Who makes the decisions?
Who else has influence?

Tracking the progress of the relationship
The eight-stage process
Using consulting skills
Measures of success

Putting it into practice
Providing the opportunity to practise the skills and to receive feedback

Improving the relationship
Marketing
Communications
Administration
Measuring client satisfaction

Next steps
Action planning
Review the outcomes and success criteria

MENTORING

Mentoring is less proactive than coaching. Mentors are normally senior people who offer support to individuals in the organization. This support is normally given when requested. Therefore mentors are often offered to individuals when they join an organization as a source of support throughout their career. The shoestring manager either performs that role themselves, or helps the organization to identify and train suitable senior managers.

The mentor can be used as a means of helping individuals identify their training needs, or in providing a sounding board for individuals to talk through their career development.

In a shoestring environment mentors are even more valuable both as a support to you but also as the 'glue' that can hold an organization together at times of change. Well chosen and trained mentors can help smooth some of the difficulties of transition. Often at times of change unhelpful rumours are started by people concerned for the security of their own job, or who do not like the proposed changes. Having mentors strategically available within the organization who can just talk honestly and openly to people about the realities of organizational change can be a very powerful tool.

The skill set is very similar to coaching: mentors often take corporate messages and concepts and translate them into information which is more easily assimilated. They need to be attentive listeners, and to provide reassurance and a positive role model.

FACILITATION

One of the roles the shoestring manager can perform, or contract in, is that of facilitator for change. In this role you are attempting to help the organization understand itself by stepping back and reflecting. In many ways you would need to develop the skill set of a business process facilitator.

There are some key skills and knowledge involved in this role:

❏ listening skills,

❏ understanding of group dynamics,

❏ the ability to challenge constructively and to encourage and support,

❏ a knowledge of the companies' aims and goals.

Operating as a facilitator for change, you are looking to establish the issues for the group. You are moving from a process of seeking information through encouraging the group to formulate its own solutions, to getting them to stand on their own two feet.

The key components are:

❏ questioning

❏ challenging

❏ encouraging

❏ supporting.

The process can best be illustrated by the continuum shown in Figure 5.

At the beginning you are more likely to be asking questions. You will challenge assumptions in order to get the participants to step back and view their own processes. During the early phase you will encourage new ideas and risk-taking, and support decisions to do things differently.

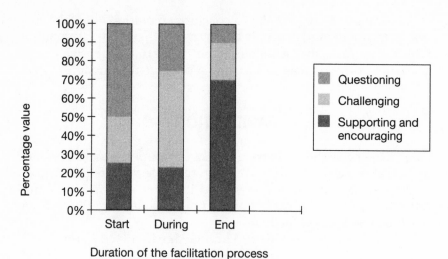

Figure 5 Facilitation: the process continuum.

As the group begins to question its own processes your role as inquisitor diminishes, but your willingness to challenge remains. The group now needs your encouragement and support.

The whole idea of your role is to eventually wean the group away from dependence on your interventions to make decisions without you. Therefore in the final phase it would not be unusual for your actions to be more about support and encouragement with a little challenging and then the questioning.

In summary you move from *making* decisions for the group to joining the group decision making process and ending with the group making its own decisions.Depending on your role and experience you may undertake this work yourself, or work with a strategic consultant to facilitate in a more formal process. To work at this level you should consider further training.

Although you may not feel equipped to operate initially at this strategic level you may feel more confident to facilitate at an implementation level. In this context the shoestring manager can perform a really important role. Some issues in an organization do not need a training solution, instead, teams need to think creatively around a problem or to brainstorm possible solutions.

As a facilitator the shoestring manager needs to follow a particular process and you need to develop facilitating skills.

A good facilitator needs to be able to:

- [ ] take an overview of the situation;

- [ ] identify individual and organizational needs;

- [ ] use a variety of interpersonal skills to enable individuals and teams to contribute;

- [ ] use tools and techniques to work through a process to reach a conclusion;

- [ ] gain commitment to action;

- [ ] record any outcomes;

- [ ] follow up and review the process.

How to facilitate

Step 1: Identify your target audience
Who is involved?
What level are they in the company?
How do they relate to you?
How much do you know about them?
What is their style and approach?
What could be the differences, or points of conflict?

Step 2: Identify the targeted outcome
What are you trying to achieve?
What would be a satisfying conclusion?
Who has an interest in the outcome?

Step 3: Prepare for the event
Think about your style.
Practise listening and questioning.
Think about appropriate open questions.
Think about the structure of the event.
Have people been notified of the event?
Have you circulated an agenda with the detail of the proposed structure of the day, and the outcomes where known?

Step 4: Tools and techniques
Although facilitation may seem a very natural process of helping individuals and groups to reach a conclusion there are a number of tools and techniques which can help the process. We detail a number of them at the end of this chapter.

Step 5: Gain commitment to action, record any outcomes
Help the group to reach appropriate conclusions. Record any decisions taken.

Sometimes the stages taken to reach the conclusion, ie flipcharts, SWOTs, Mind Maps, etc are useful to keep.

Encourage the group to set out action lists with details of action to be taken, by whom, and by when.

Step 6 : Review the process
After the event, it will be important to go back and review the outcomes and to monitor progress.

Shoestring checklist

✓ Develop an enhanced skill set in the key skills.

✓ Use the eight-stage checklist.

✓ Look at each technique and assess your own competence.

✓ Do the same for any team members that you have.

✓ Think about your role: which tools or techniques would be helpful in your work?

✓ Identify a mentor for yourself and arrange to meet regularly.

FRAMEWORK OF TECHNIQUES

We are not including a large section on designing training as there are a number of books on the market which deal with this topic including our companion book. However we have included at the end of this section some sample sessions, including the 30-minute solution which is based on how service organizations deliver training, and is very focused. We anticipate the shoestring manager will use internal or external providers to design and deliver the training for them, using the eight-stage process that we described in Chapter 3. We have, however, included some of the key techniques that you might use as a facilitator or internal consultant. They are as relevant to a problem solving session within a business as a training session.

BRAINSTORMING

This is one of the simplest yet most effective techniques for working with groups. Using a blank piece of flipchart paper and a single topic or heading, you note as many ideas as possible that are generated by your participants. The technique is designed to help with the flow of ideas and there are important rules, eg no editing, no qualifying, no restricting. The concept works because one person's thoughts often stimulates others and, by not interrupting each other, the ideas flow very quickly. Analysis can take place later.

SWOT (STRENGTHS, WEAKNESSES, OPPORTUNITIES, THREATS)

This is a way of adding structure to a brainstorm. By dividing a piece of flipchart paper into four and adding the headings Strengths, Weaknesses, Opportunities and Threats, a group may analyse their business, the workings of their team, future business potential or any other aspect of the organization as seems appropriate. Strengths and weaknesses are often perceived as current and internal, and threats as future and external issues.

MIND MAPPING

Tony Buzan invented mind mapping. The usage is endless: note-taking, problem solving, decision making, planning and designing training. One of the great advantages is that large amounts of information can be summarized on one page. It is a very visual process.

To get the best from mind maps he recommends the following:

1. Use a plain piece of paper to draw a coloured image or write a word in the middle of the page.

2. Leaving the mind as free as possible, brainstorm your ideas. At this stage do not worry too much about sequencing or order, the key is to capture thoughts as quickly as possible.

3. Words should be in units, one word to a line

4. Words should be printed in capitals. The printed words should be on the line and each line should be connected to other lines. This ensures the basic structure.

5. Use of illustrations and colour can also help in the process.

6. It is something that can be started by one person and then shared with another to build ideas.

7. Further information is available from Tony Buzan (see Recommended Reading at the end of the book).

CARD SORTS

Similar to brainstorming, this technique allows individuals to write their thoughts on small pieces of card or sticky notes, then the facilitator helps the participant to group similar issues or points under headings. Each person writes their own response, the smallness of paper helping them focus their thoughts, and during feedback the ideas are clustered under appropriate headings. The ideas can also be moved into new combinations under different headings. The advantage of this method is that everyone can make a contribution. It gives the more reflective thinkers time to assimilate their thoughts. It does need some careful pulling together of everyone's ideas at the end of the process.

ROLE PLAY

Role play is a powerful tool to help people experience different situations in a 'safe' environment. There are specific ways that role play should be structured.

There are normally three roles :

1. An active person – the one with the key role, eg a coach.

2. A partner – the person playing a support role, eg a person being coached.

3. An observer – the person who will observe the role-play activity and who will give helpful feedback on performance.

The scenarios are normally developed before the event, and like the case studies described below should relate to the normal situation that the active person would later be putting into practice. So for example if it was a role play about coaching, the active person could be a line manager practising coaching one of his team. Role plays can be generated spontaneously as part of an event; most people have had experiences that they would like to re-run, but it will still need a structure to ensure the role play runs smoothly.

In either case time needs to be allowed for preparation. Timings are normally as follows:

❑ 15–20 minutes preparation,

❑ 15–20 minutes for each role play,

❑ 10 minutes feedback.

The key to successful role-playing is recognizing that it is more about improvisation than acting. There may be an outline script to help people get started, but once they are in the role play then they should use their own natural responses. They should be encouraged to try different techniques so that they explore the whole of their skill set.

The partner should play their role as realistically as possible to help the active person practise their skills, but again they should avoid overacting. If the active person is doing really well they could increase the pressure a little, perhaps by including some more 'difficult' behaviours.

The observer's role is key, and belies the description 'observer'. It is not a chance to sit back and switch off. The observer must stay back out of the action, but nonetheless record key statements, body language and behaviours to enable them to give effective feedback on the performances at the end of the role play.

They should observe the rules of good feedback which are:

❑ Start with a positive non threatening opening.

❑ Ask the active person how they felt about their performance first.

❑ Ask the partner how realistic they felt it was for them.

❑ Use questions to stimulate ownership and discussion.

❑ Give specific examples.

❑ Not too many points.

❑ End with the positive.

Role plays should normally be undertaken with a level of privacy ie in triads in separate rooms, or at least separate spaces. It is also important to explain that you are trying to create a 'safe' environment to enable people to practise their skills, and so they should not discuss individual performances once the role play is over.

CASE STUDIES

Like role plays, case studies are designed to enable participants to explore the 'what ifs' of a situation. The case studies are normally prepared before an event and are based on examples which bear close relation to actual situations that the participants have to deal with in their normal working environment. They should not be identified as real people, but can include similar characteristics.

Instead of role play, what normally happens is that people work in teams to identify potential solutions to the situations or issues raised. Again it gives people the opportunity to re-run history, show how they can troubleshoot and problem solve, and demonstrate working in teams. This technique can also be used to project behaviours into the future by being given the opportunity to look at some future business opportunity, for example, 'If we were going to move our distribution centre, where would you site it and why?' 'Which of our products could we export?'

The key is to encourage the groups to use a variety of the techniques that we highlight above and use their own creativity to generate new approaches. These types of events could be part of a series of short input sessions over a period of time and could open up the channels of communication to senior management where appropriate so that people feel that their ideas are being valued. These sessions could also become part of the regular business development.

TEAM BUILDING

One of the key areas of development for many organizations is team building. In streamlined organizations team leadership and team membership become important areas of focus. As part of this process individuals also need personal feedback. There are a number of ways of doing this including assessment/development centres or psychometric tests, but whichever route is chosen the more feedback that individuals receive the more comfortable and confident they will be with themselves, and the more effective they will be in teams.

In shoestring environments one of the frustrating factors is the ineffectiveness of teams.Therefore it is important to support teams in the establishment of effective team processes. This is a classic example of where the shoestring manager could facilitate the team in identifying the criteria for effective meetings. This could be undertaken with a management team at any level. Once they have identified how to generate the right criteria they could then use the same process with their teams to agree a procedure for running meetings, again gaining commitment and buy-in from the team members. Thus without a long training process some key skill transfer will take place.

Creating a team environment does not necessarily involve residential team-building events. Encouraging people to meet socially, creating a supportive work environment, facilitating meetings where senior management work with their teams in solving operational issues, are just as effective learning processes. Key to making this work is encouraging senior management in the sharing of the vision and values and being honest and open in relationships.

THE 30-MINUTE SOLUTION

As we discussed in the introduction there are a number of ways that training can be delivered. In this example we show how even in quite small amounts of time key messages can be transmitted if the training is well organized.

For many years in retailing and in some cases in banking you would see a note on the door,

'Monday closed for staff training 9.00–9.30'

Having reviewed some of the training plans behind these 30-minute sessions a number of things become clear:

❏ Very clear objectives were set at the start of the session.

❏ The session tended to focus on one critical aspect of training.

❏ Wandering from the topic was actively discouraged.

❏ Key points were summarized, sometimes with a checklist summary card, or if the session formed part of an ongoing training session they were encouraged to refer to additional points in their workbook.

❏ There was a clear direction to the staff trainer, 'Introduce no new points at this stage, prepare staff to return to the shop floor.'

A range of media might be used in the training, for example:

❏ an icebreaker

❏ a video

❏ a game

❏ a presenter.

Therefore if you were following the same process with your training the same principles would apply.

SAMPLE SESSION

Icebreaker: very quick round the table response, name one thing you could do with a plastic card...

Introduce today's topic: LOYALTY CARDS

The objectives are: by the end of this session you will be able to;

❑ Adopt a customer-service approach to the use of loyalty cards.

❑ Put into practice the technical training that you have received.

Show *video:* video highlights the key steps in the process, and reminds the participants of the key messages that they have to give to the customer.

Ask each member of the group to describe a feature or benefit of using the loyalty card.

Write the pneumonic on the flipchart :

❑ **Lasting**

❑ **Offer**

❑ **You'll**

❑ **Always**

❑ **Love**

Issue the checklist card.

Check if there are any questions.

Remind the group of the topic for next week's session, and the current focus phrase.

Send them back to the shop floor on time.

Shoestring checklist

✓ Think about the 'big picture'.

✓ Use the techniques that are appropriate to your group.

✓ Practise in a 'safe' environment.

✓ Observe other people using them, learn from them.

✓ Use your common sense, do not be seduced into situations where you feel uncomfortable, just because someone says it is a 'good 'learning experience!

✓ Learn from others, ask for help and advice.

Thinking outside the square

In Chapters 3 and 4 we have primarily explored some traditional routes to identifying and delivering a training solution. In this chapter we explore some alternatives.

NOT OFFERING FORMAL TRAINING

Not every learning need will be met by offering a training solution. Increasingly, businesses are wanting to experiment with other options. We discussed coaching in Chapter 4, which has been adopted by many organizations as a way not only of developing individual and line management skills, but also of contributing to the creation of a more thoughtful organizational environment.

CONTINUOUS PROFESSIONAL DEVELOPMENT

With increasing emphasis on transfer of skills and mobility, more and more organizations and individuals are focusing on the importance of continuing professional development. This takes many forms: open learning, attendance at short courses, further and higher education. As a shoestring manager you may be identifying opportunities for yourself or your colleagues.

Important questions to ask are:

1. What do I/you hope to gain by pursuing this route?

2. Where can I do it?

3. Who else has done it that I know?

4. How did they find it worked?

5. Can I afford it?

6. Will the company sponsor it?

7. What will the company gain as a result of it?

8. Have I got a support mechanism to help me through it?

9. Do I really want to do it? Why?

Some of the higher level qualifications such as an MBA or PhD really do require an enormous amount of personal dedication. However for the individual they are a source of networking, benchmarking, personal achievement, recognition and satisfaction. For the shoestring organization they are a way of importing new and innovative ideas into the business, and a source of strategic consultancy support.

If you are considering this type of investment it is critically important to shop around to find the best possible provider in terms of location, support and the structure of the course. Your checklist for selection could include:

❑ The award is accredited by a professional body.

❑ The provider is a recognized Centre of Excellence.

❑ It has perceived value within your organization.

❑ This is balanced against geographical location/cost.

❑ The award is current and is regularly updated.

❑ Both the award and the centre are respected within your industry.

❑ It may help you to become eligible for sponsorship.

SECONDMENT

This is another way of developing individuals. It is a method that has been successfully used in education for many years, where teachers or lecturers spend time in other learning environments. This may be an international exchange, or within a corporate organization, before returning to their own establishment and sharing what they had learnt with their colleagues.

Businesses too are using this approach, through Head Office staff visiting the field and vice versa. In some cases this has been structured into an induction or graduate programmes.

In other cases it has become part of a formal commitment that senior managers will spend time working in the field. The shoe-string manager can support this process by helping people to recognize the learning that has taken place. Then either through the setting of objectives, or as a part of a personal development plan, encourage people to record their learnings from the process.

The secondment will be a more powerful learning experience if the following takes place:

❑ There is a link with organization goals, skills and competencies.

❑ It makes links with goals, skills and competencies in other organizations.

❑ Clear learning objectives are set.

❑ Work shadowing can be considered as a means of gaining a perspective over a specific period of time.

❑ Debriefing takes place on return to parent organization.

Secondment can be used to gain experience in topics not covered in the parent organization, for example finance, or marketing at micro level, or new product strategy at macro level. There may also be specific occasions when you can gain experience: every time a meeting takes place with a different part of the business, or you visit a new business or educational establishment, learning takes place.

Having identified that secondment is of interest to you or a person that you are working with, how do you achieve it?

1. Talk to the relevant senior management, either your own line manager, or someone who has the ability to make it happen. If

this is part of a more significant secondment, either on an international scale, or if it involves board sign-off then the process may take longer.

2. Build it into your personal development plan (PDP) (see below and Chapter 8).

3. Identify interesting projects which already exist and that have a particular interest for you.

4. Network within the business and elsewhere to identify potential opportunities.

5. Think about other opportunities outside the immediate spectrum of your working environment.

6. Think positively about how the secondment could fit within the overall development of the business.

PERSONAL DEVELOPMENT PLANS

PDPs can be a sophisticated tool linking to organization goals, competencies and appraisal systems. However to ensure their ongoing success it is important to ensure that support is given to and from line managers.

PDPs are a very powerful mechanism that the shoestring manager can introduce or harness as part of the organizational training plan. Helping people keep track of their own development can be a significant factor in career progression. It need not involve a large investment in training, but introduced properly and supported by coaching from line management it can provide a source of ongoing learning for everyone, which requires minimum investment in training and ensures that when a training need is identified it is as the result of a sensible discussion between the learner and his manager.

The only financial investment required to introduce PDPs may be the production of a folder and a structured series of questions to help the individual and his manager identify objectives and courses of action to take them through the next few months (see Appendix 5 for example of PDP layout). However the real time cost of line managers sitting down with their team members to review their PDPs does need to be taken into consideration, as does the training of line managers.

Although the introduction may seem comparatively simple,

there are also dangers in publishing PDPs and then leaving the participant to sink or swim.

The shoestring manager needs to gain commitment from and involve senior management in the launch.There should also be briefing sessions for line managers on how to introduce and maintain the process.

The shoestring manager then needs to monitor the progress and to encourage line managers to provide feedback on the coaching support offered.They also need to identify where specific training needs have been identified.

The advantage of this process is that it provides a continuous infrastructure of development that is owned by the business and often increases individual motivation because of the increased contact between the individual and their line manager. It is likely that the process will need to be supported by the development of coaching skills in line managers.

ACTION LEARNING

When considering training solutions you may want something that is going to provide an ongoing solution which helps staff develop processes to deal with the next problem that comes along. Action Learning might be the training solution you are looking for.

Action Learning is an approach to management training developed by Professor Reg Revans. The purpose of this technique is to provide managers with the skills to analyse problems by using their experience to produce credible solutions, and to develop techniques to anticipate and handle change. At its simplest, this training solution periodically brings together a group (or Set) of managers to work on real life organizational issues. The group has available a Set Advisor who acts more as a facilitator than a trainer, to help them focus on the Action Learning process.

An Action Learning programme has four basic steps:

1. Each delegate is asked to write a brief description of the change problem to be tackled, and a picture of how things will be when this problem is resolved, together with an identification of what benefits will result. This problem must be a live issue for the delegate who is committed to taking action.

2. Problems are then described to the group. Other members help each person to learn from their actions by questions and feed-

back, support and challenge. A Set Advisor helps the group to manage the process and encourages members to give and take between themselves.

3. As a result of the discussions each delegate is encouraged to reflect on their individual problem and to plan a course of action on their return to the office. Before leaving, the members agree a schedule of half-day meetings every four to six weeks.

4. At these set meetings members share time and report in turn on their efforts since the last meeting. As before, members will be encouraged to give and take between themselves. Finally, each person ends by setting goals for action to be carried out by the next meeting.

This is a simple yet profound process. Only individuals prepared to take a risk and commit themselves to action and reflection will be able to learn in this way. A key feature of the action learning process is that participants are enabled to learn from each other. Revans has described Set members as 'comrades in adversity'.

Action Learning Sets bring together small groups of managers with the following intentions:

❑ To undertake to work on and through management problems.

❑ To work on real problems with which they are actively engaged.

❑ Situations in which 'I am part of the problem and the problem is part of me.'

❑ To work together to check individual perceptions, clarify (and render more manageable) the problem, and to explore alternatives for action.

❑ To take action in the light of new insight. This will begin to change the situation and an account of the consequences will be brought back to the group for further shared reflection.

❑ To focus on learning, not only about the problem being tackled but also on what is being learned about oneself. This is essential if developing understanding is to become learning and thus transferable to other situations.

❑ To be aware of group processes and to develop effective ways of working together. Each group is provided with a facilitator whose role is to help the group to identify and develop the necessary skills.

❑ To provide the balance of support and challenge which will enable each individual to manage more effectively.

It may be tempting for delegates to choose an issue which they have already partly solved, but in practice this will offer little challenge and will defeat the idea of action learning. Action Learning is more effective when applied to an open ended problem rather than a close ended problem or puzzle. An open ended problem is more difficult to handle since it is influenced by many factors, has more possible solutions and no clear cut answers. They are more complex and are dealt with by different individuals in different ways. A puzzle on the other hand, has a unique solution, which can be found if a problem-solving technique is properly applied, or by using experts.

The Problem Action Sheet in Appendix 3 will help your Set focus on the issues and the process of Action Learning.

SETTING UP YOUR OWN LEARNING RESOURCE CENTRE

The shoestring manager may consider the setting up of a learning resource centre as a different way of allocating the training budget. One of the important first steps is to thoroughly analyse the costs involved in the process. A source of help in undertaking this is *Learning Centres* by Amanda Scott published by Kogan Page, which is a step-by-step guide to the setting up and managing of a corporate learning resource centre.

Within this text she reviews a number of key stages in setting up a centre. Of particular interest to the shoestring manager is a section on getting the best from a small or 'compact' learning centre. She suggests making such a centre available to individual departments at a particular time almost as a pilot, so that if it is successful you can ask for additional funds to expand the centre.

She suggests that the format of these smaller learning centres contain smaller texts such as the *Better Management Skills* series from Kogan Page, or *Management Pocket Books* from Melrose. Computer based packages, audio tapes and training videos can form the basis of such a centre. She also suggests that charities can obtain discounts from publishers and promotional material can also be obtained free to improve the appearance of such a centre.

However it is also important to remember the support needed when using this type of material. Learners need someone to discuss their learning needs with and to provide coaching support. If as we discussed in Chapters 3 and 4 you have trained line managers in coaching skills they can discuss with their individual team members their training needs and then select the appropriate learning support material.

To make the learning even more effective it is important to keep the learning centre up to date, and to ensure that the learners are able to use the material properly. It may be helpful to provide guidance notes on the use of the centre and to encourage participants to analyse their learning style to help them make best use of the facilities.

This is a role that the shoestring manager may be able to perform depending on your workload, or you may appoint a learning advisor whose role is to support managers as they manage the interface between the workplace and the learning centre. You may also need administrative support to ensure the ongoing availability of materials and the smooth running of the centre.

Finally, a word on the environment. In the past, resources like those in some in-company training rooms may not have been in the most conducive of environments. If you have a limited budget think very carefully about the following:

❑ seating

❑ lighting

❑ temperature

❑ space

❑ noise level

❑ target audience

❑ security.

You do not need an enormous room, but try and find somewhere which allows for a range of working and seating arrangements, somewhere where people feel comfortable in.

It is also important to remember that individuals have different learning styles, and as a result the learning resource centre approach may not be suitable for all learners.

LEARNING RESOURCES

As we discussed in several of our earlier chapters, people learn in different ways, and when you are training on a shoestring you need to consider a wide variety of learning methods and approaches. There is still a lot of confusion about the various terms involved in learning resources. Even without setting up formal learning centres the shoestring manager needs to consider the use of different learning techniques.

In Chapter 3 and 4 we explored the more traditional forms of training and development; in this chapter we are looking at a variety of ways of learning using new technology. One very important factor to consider is the speed of change in new technology, and this must also be judged against the level of investment that you are considering.

First, it is important to understand the different terms and what form of learning it provides; we are also conscious that the terms used have a different interpretation in different parts of the world!

Broadly then, this is what is meant by the following terms:

DISTANCE LEARNING

Distance learning normally takes place at a distance from the designer or presenter of the material. One early example of this was correspondence courses, which were primarily written text, and often presented the learner with an opportunity of gaining qualifications. In today's working environments they present an option which means that the learner does not have to attend a training centre, but can learn at a time, pace and place which suits their own learning needs. The original text-based material has now been supplemented by a range of other media, either audio, video, CBT, CD-ROM, Internet and also by tutorial support.

Distance learning is often used as a means of gaining a qualification. Many universities have adopted this method as a way of supporting continuing professional development.

OPEN LEARNING

Open learning means ease of access, there are no barriers to stop anyone learning. Like distance learning, open learning allows the learner to learn at a time, place and pace to suit their needs. Open learning often makes use of text, audio, video, and Computer Based Training (CBT). In the UK the Open University was one of the first and enduringly successful exponents of this type of learning. As technology advances methods such as CD-ROM and e-mail have been included. These offer more interaction, and possibilities for networking with other learners.

Each of these methods present the learner with an alternative to direct training or coaching. The success of this method really does depend on the right training needs analysis, and support being available.

DIAGNOSTICS

New technology can help individuals gain a clearer understanding of themselves. We have already discussed encouraging learners to identify their learning style, but increasingly other forms of analysis are becoming available through different packages. Individuals can work through PC based packages to gain a better understanding of their skills, personality and team behaviours. This will also need to be supported by review and feedback with a line manager or coach. The more sophisticated packages will generate profiles which can then be used to develop personal development plans.

COMPUTER BASED TRAINING (CBT)

Computer based packages have in fact been available for a considerable time, though the understanding of their effective use is much more recent.

Samuel A. Malone in *How to Set up and Manage a Corporate Learning Centre* suggests that CBT caters for different learning styles and he says:

> Research into how people learn and remember suggests that we retain about 20% of what we hear, 40% of what we see and hear, and 75% of what we see, hear and do. Multimedia engages all the

senses, hearing, seeing and doing – and thus maximizes learning while catering for every learning style.

He goes on to suggest that: 'comparative studies suggest that learning effectiveness of CBT is superior to conventional training – people learn faster and retain more- some studies showing an improvement in the time required to learn of 50%.' The reasoning behind this is due to the pace that a learner uses, and to interaction and feedback.

While there is evidence for this view, as in the ancient proverb

> I hear and I forget
> I see and I remember
> I do and I understand

it does depend on the quality of both the training and the learning resources, and as we discussed in Chapter 1, the individual's learning style.

A charismatic trainer who engages the learner in lots of practical and memorable training activities reinforced with handouts and supported by ongoing coaching or mentoring, could in fact have a more positive impact on a learner than working through a computer-based package on their own in a cramped study area.

The success of CBT and other forms of multimedia really does depend on the needs of the customer, as Amanda Scott suggests:

> If you are in an organization where the technology age is far from prevalent then perhaps you should consider a more gradual approach.Self development is one culture change, having a technology change may be more than most can cope with. You need to identify the learning styles of the individuals using the centre. If you have a lot of Theorists and Reflectors then CD Rom may not be the ideal solution.

So faced with perhaps a number of differing views about the new learning technology, what should you do?

First it is important to keep an overview, and your own learners in focus; for example, if you are working in a professional practice and one of the partners wants his team to be trained in a particular piece of legislation and a software package has been developed to specifically meet that need, then it may prove to be the best solution; particularly if the partners are prepared to act as 1–1 follow up support as required, and that there is opportunity to reinforce the learning.

If however you are working in an organization which needs to introduce a coaching culture, it would be inappropriate to make every one work through a multimedia package and then to assume that they would be competent to coach others without the opportunity to practice. The critical difference is in the structuring of the learning, so that a video and workbook, or a more sophisticated multimedia package could either be used as part of a trainer led programme, or as an introduction to coaching or to reinforce key learning.

In this instance the key to becoming competent is to practice within a safe environment such as supportive role play, to receive feedback, and then practice again, until the participant feels confident.

So using the above two scenarios as examples you can perhaps see the need to use the new technology appropriately.

Shoestring checklist

The key to success in using CBT or any multimedia package lies in identifying answers to the following:

✓ How ready are my users to adapt to using new technology?

✓ What part of my budget should I allocate to the purchase of learning resources?

✓ Do I want to simply supplement the current training offering with some selected materials, or do I want to set up a Learning Resources Centre?

✓ Are there other facilities corporately or locally, where I could use them instead of purchasing them?

✓ Is my organization ready for the introduction of new technology?

✓ Is there a supporter other than me?

✓ What hardware do we have? Is it suitable for running CBT packages, or multimedia?

> ✓ Could we fund an administrator to manage the resources?
>
> ✓ Do I really need to purchase anything? Can I ask my current suppliers to incorporate the opportunity to use different technologies within their training?
>
> ✓ Is there government funding to support the introduction of new technology?

Depending on your responses to the above questions you will either be considering setting up a learning resource centre, purchasing some materials to support your training, or perhaps negotiating with suppliers.

If you decide to purchase materials either for a centre or to supplement existing training then these are some of the questions to consider:

1. How is it presented? Is it easy to use? Are the instructions clear? This is particularly important with a more complex package.

2. Will it support the current or proposed learning initiatives? The shoestring budget will not stretch to packages that have no clear purpose.

3   Does it support the corporate culture? Often the style of the presenter, or the language in a package, or video can prompt a negative response from the learners.

4. Will it sustain interest, have you used it? You should never purchase something that you have not used, or at least viewed or seen demonstrated.

5. Is it up to date? One of the problems with some of the more traditional learning packages, particularly videos, were that they became dated very easily. Fashions, or the age of well-known presenters or actors showed the real vintage of the material. Currently this is less of an issue for multimedia material that is just being developed, but in the long term it could also be an issue.

6. Does it represent good value? What do you get for your money? Unfortunately it is possible to purchase a package

without viewing it and then when you compare your package with perhaps another one on the market you realize that you have purchased a very expensive option.

7. Is it well structured? Is it easy for the learner to use? Does it have clear objectives? Does it test understanding? Is there a logical route through?

8. How much learner support will be required? Depending on your reasons for purchasing the product, the amount of additional contact time required will be important.

9. Will it be durable, is it of good quality? It is easy to be seduced by good external packaging, but ensure that the rest of the contents will stand the test of time and are re-usable.

10. Finally, and this is a test of any corporate investment, if you were using your own money would you buy it? If so, why?

It is always helpful to have an answer to this question, because if it is your own business you have the justification for making the purchase. If you are purchasing something on behalf of an organization you need to be satisfied in your own mind that you have done the right thing.

Finally, it is important to remember you are not alone when considering the purchase of materials; we will discuss networking and benchmarking in Chapter 6. Always use your contacts for their opinion, particularly for the major purchases. Remember to ask advice from the producers of the material, or specialist learning resource centre staff.

Using outside support

NETWORKING

The shoestring manager's role can be a lonely one particularly if your individual circumstances have changed and colleagues have either left or moved into other roles. This is why networking is so important. If you have a responsibility for the development of others it is important that you take time to develop yourself and also to keep up to date with T&D initiatives.

One very cost effective way of doing this is through networking. Many informal networks exist around the country, where people meet either through professional associations or through informal networks to share best practice.

Sources of networks can be:

❑ former business colleagues,

❑ contacts from other companies or institutions who are in your business or education sector,

❑ social contacts who are involved in business or education,

❑ local business groups and trade associations.

You may find that you are targeted to join a network, or you may wish to establish a network based on your own particular interest.

BENCHMARKING

Benchmarking is a technique that has grown in popularity as a way of sharing information among organizations and professionals. You can benchmark almost anything. There is a process of structuring the questions to obtain the information that you want. Essentially data will either be quantitative which is data related or qualitative which is based on opinions and views. Your network may well be willing to include you in their benchmarking surveys, or they may be willing to take part in yours.

Secondment

We discussed this in detail in Chapter 5, but it is an important concept to keep in mind, as it can be a powerful way of finding out more about your organization, or other environments.

MEMBERSHIP OF PROFESSIONAL ASSOCIATIONS

As we discussed above, it is important to keep up to date with the latest developments in your profession. This is even more important if you have limited resources. There are associations for personnel and training professionals in most countries, as well as specialist associations for different market sectors. The shoestring manager needs to look carefully at the cost of membership versus the services provided. Questions to ask are:

❑ What do I get for my subscription fee, eg publications, access to libraries, reading lists, resources, etc?

❑ Are there meetings or events that I can attend locally or nationally?

❑ What other benefits are there associated with joining, eg other discounts or accredited training?

❑ Will my organization pay the fee? Should we become corporate members

❑ What are the advantages?

❑ How will I justify this fee?

SUBSCRIPTIONS TO PUBLICATIONS

The decisions about subscriptions to publications are similar to that of membership of any association. The key question is: what do you get for your fee? Always ask for samples of the journals before paying for anything. Make a practical assessment based on the quality of articles, currency of information and number of issues per year. Always find out if you are eligible for free subscription. In many cases trade journals are free to those working in a particular sector. Always explore other avenues: does your local library stock copies? Does anyone else in your organization subscribe to the same publication? Ask their opinion, explore the possibility of sharing copies.

LEARNING RESOURCE CENTRES

We discussed setting up a resource centre in Chapter 5, but as well as considering the setting up of your own centre there are other options. A source of external support are learning resource centres.These broadly take two forms: (1) Commercial centres from which you can view and then purchase or hire materials. (2) In-company centres where individual learners can use resources as part of their personal development.

Commercial centres

The aim of the commercial centre is to provide information about a wide range of resources. These centres offer advice in the whole area of resource based learning. They will help in the setting up of internal learning centres, advising on the purchase of both hardware and software and other resources. They will normally have premises where you can view and use resources and order your own selection of materials.

Producers of videos and other learning materials also arrange exhibitions or special previews of their materials and may sponsor other viewing centres. The advantage of all of these services is that you do not need to purchase anything until you are absolutely certain that it is right for your organization.

Always negotiate for special offers wherever possible, and check about discounting arrangements.

Internal learning centres

Increasingly, organizations are considering setting up their own learning centres to house the type of materials that we discussed in Chapter 5. It is important that a learning centre should not just be set up to house materials. It is a different approach to learning and as such you need to budget not just for the hardware and resources, but the running costs of the centre, administrators, and the ongoing marketing and promotion. If you are interested in viewing such a centre, use your network to identify the organizations who may have their own learning centre, and ask if you may view it.

LIBRARIES

We can often ignore the simple concepts in our search for the more sophisticated solutions. Libraries, particularly city, university or business school libraries often have tremendous sources of information. Equally, professional associations often offer a library service. In each case they often have access to interesting data bases which may provide you with information about grants and other initiatives.They will do searches for you, and they usually have a great love of research and information.

PRODUCERS AND SUPPLIERS OF MATERIALS

With the growth of resource based learning more and more sources of materials are becoming available.A resourceful shoestring manager will make contact with such publishers. There are many reasons for this:

❑ access to review copies,

❑ piloting or testing of materials,

❑ keeping up-to-date with new releases,

❑ invitations to new product launches or exhibitions.

It is very easy to be put on a mailing list. Review any training journal and you will be able to identify a number of producers of resources who you can contact and then on a regular basis you will be sent catalogues, other promotional material and invitations to product launches. This will also have the additional benefit of benchmarking other suppliers and meeting other training professionals.

In evaluating materials you need to consider the following:

❑ flexibility,

❑ ease of usage,

❑ value for money,

❑ linkage to work situation,

❑ ongoing reliability.

TRAINING PROVIDERS

As well as information from producers and suppliers of material, another source of useful information are training providers. What you may want to do is identify a number of key organizations and ask to go on their mailing list. This will be particularly important if you plan to use open programmes as a source of training for your people. Equally if you wish to use external training consultants to provide some of your in-house training you need to select appropriate partners.

Although it is an investment of time you should regularly review your current providers and give other consultancies the opportunity to meet with you and to discuss your requirements.

CHOOSING AN EXTERNAL TRAINING CONSULTANT

External training consultants are often used when:

❑ You have no internal resources.

❑ There is a need for a small number of highly specialized programmes.

❑ Internal resources are fully committed to high priority programmes.

When it is agreed with the programme's sponsor, an external view with experience from outside your organization, will significantly contribute to the success of your programme.

PREPARING A BRIEF

You may have a set procedure for procuring external services, which may relate to the numbers of organizations invited to send in proposals, the fees, or the process.

However, to help an external organization work with you the following points need to be considered:

1. Invite more than one provider to present to you.

2. Give a clear specification for the required task, or activity; set success criteria.

3. Set the scene, brief the provider on the background to the organization and the business outcomes you are working towards (only share information which is not commercially sensitive).

4. Give a clear indication of the timescale and any other relevant information.

5. Check references, either from within your own organization or elsewhere, look for demonstrable experience in the knowledge or skill areas.

6. Ensure that you meet the people that you will be working with, not just the senior directors. Check their interpersonal skills; could you work with this person or organization?

WORKING WITH EXTERNAL PROVIDERS

Maintain close contact with the work – ensure that it is progressing on time and that the feedback from the users is positive.

1. Do everything you can to ensure that they fit into the organization. Help them to understand the culture and any jargon.

2. Share everything that is relevant to do with the project; its background, how it links with other initiatives, any issues, any areas of resistance.

3. Identify any members of the internal team and provide an

organization chart and if appropriate organize introductions or brief meetings with key people.

4. Monitor performance, review any evaluations.

5. Revisit the original brief at the end of the project: have the success criteria been met?

6. Always treat outside providers fairly

We highlight in the Foreword and in Chapter 8 the need for the shoestring manager to practice good time and priority management. To implement any of the suggestions in this chapter will involve some allocation of time. As part of your overview you need to identify your priorities and to include the above suggestions as appropriate. For example if you plan to attend one training exhibition a year choose the one which gives you the widest selection of materials.

If you cannot justify the fee to attend a particular training conference enquire about purchasing the notes from the event. If you wish to subscribe to a training journal explore membership of a training institute which includes subscription to a training journal.

If you have a specialist interest in a particular subject can you be a guest speaker at a conference? Not only is it a great learning experience but if you are successful you will become a good ambassador for your organization and you will have the opportunity to meet other people.

VENUES

The shoestring manager may need to use external facilities to provide a base for their training. If you are looking for an external venue you need to think creatively about what facilities you may want to hire. It can, however, provide additional facilities that you may not have within your own environment.

Do not automatically assume that these venues need to be hotels or conference centres; many organizations are now hiring out their premises at very cost-effective rates. You really need to explore the options locally and again this is where your network can be a very useful source of information.

Equally, within your own organization explore what space is available. With open plan offices being created, previous dedicated office space may become available. This may become the base for a learning resource centre, or utilized for some of the smaller training programmes that you need to run.

When hiring external facilities always negotiate; never accept the first price offered. Think about the duration of the programmes, think about ways of creatively combining accommodation and day delegate rates, or providing your own equipment.

One word of warning: be very careful about the provision of food and refreshments. Although it is possible to make savings by reducing the choice of food at lunchtime or the size of the room, this may have a negative effect on the response to the day from the participants.

Shoestring checklist

✓ Look outwards not inwards.

✓ Learn from others, make the most of their expertise.

✓ Share information (non-sensitive)with others and they will do the same for you.

✓ Look outside the obvious.

✓ Extend your range of experience.

✓ Use benchmarking as a way of monitoring your own development as well as others.

Evaluating the results

As mentioned in Chapter 1, evaluation of training should be regarded as an integral part of the whole process and not tacked on as a last minute addition. A healthy approach is to adopt a policy that whenever a decision is taken to meet a training need, plans should also be drawn up to evaluate that training. Not to do so will leave you vulnerable to irrational reactions which cannot be verified either for or against. A key principle should be that the training provided should be of higher value to the organization than the resources needed to provide that training.

We assume that the purpose of evaluating training for the shoe-string training managers is threefold:

1. To convince stakeholders (including yourself and participants) of the worth of the training to the organization.

2. To involve line managers in the training process.

3. To provide information about the effectiveness of the training design and delivery.

There might be others you could use, but we think these are the ones that will have the highest priority.

SETTING UP THE MEASUREMENTS – THE STRATEGY

There was a time when stakeholders would accept the cost of training as an overhead without much thought about whether they were getting value for money. Those days are a thing of the past. Such blind leaps of faith are being replaced by hard-nosed decisions about the use of scarce resources. It is therefore essential in a business environment which is seeking hard data, to be systematic in developing your evaluation strategy. Although intuition and gut feeling may have their place they are less likely to convince stakeholders to initially invest in your training project nor re-invest in further projects. Through your evaluation programme you are looking to produce credible evidence which will demonstrate the value of the training to key stakeholders.

Being systematic does not necessarily mean complex. Unless it is stakeholder requirement, you are unlikely to be asked to produce information reliant on mathematical formulae in the way some academic research demands. Your evaluation strategy needs to be grounded in the reality of your organization. As explored in Chapter 1, you will have established what are the expected outcomes of the training and the related success criteria.

In agreeing the success criteria it is likely you have started to build a picture of the information needed by the stakeholders. The character of this data falls into two categories, hard and soft. Hard data characteristics are:

❑ quantifiable information such as statistical analysis and the ability of individuals to complete tasks/processes;

❑ may already be collected by existing systems in your organization;

❑ examples of hard data include error rates, turnover costs, and performance figures;

❑ examples of data measurement include regular monitoring and external benchmarking.

Be aware that should your organizations have established information systems, the data you use must be relevant to your training outcomes.

Soft data characteristics include:

❑ informed judgements and opinions of stakeholders on the significance of the training;

❑ issues such as morale, motivation and confidence which in turn have indirect influences on hard data issues such as staff turnover, sick absence levels and error rates;

❑ examples of data measurement include customer and employee surveys.

Do not make the mistake that because this type of information is less tangible that it is less important than hard data. However, be careful to ensure any soft data you use keeps in touch with reality.

It is important from the outset to agree with your principal stakeholders what you are going to measure. There are two approaches: cost benefit analysis, and cost effective analysis. The first quantifies whether the benefits of the training are more valuable to the organization in real terms than the actual costs. The second attempts to compare the costs involved with alternative ways of meeting the same training needs; for example comparing distance learning with a residential course with a workplace day course.

Broadly speaking, training costs can be divided into two categories: design costs and delivery costs, although some will be common to both.

Design costs will include items such as:

❑ accommodation including offices and perhaps training rooms;

❑ office equipment (computers, photocopiers, etc);

❑ hire/purchase of training equipment (OHPs, flip charts, etc);

❑ stationery and other consumables;

❑ trainers salaries;

❑ travel and subsistence;

❑ production of training material;

❑ analysis (needs and evaluation) questionnaires ;

❑ consultants fees;

❑ staff costs of stakeholders involved in the design and evaluation processes.

Delivery costs will include items such as:

❑ proportion of delegates salaries while undertaking the training;

❑ accommodation including training rooms and hotels if training is residential;

❑ travel costs;

❑ guest speakers' expenses (and proportion of salary if internal to organization);

❑ cost of temporary replacement staff;

❑ cost (where possible) of loss of efficiency due to absence from duties.

The availability of this information will depend on the structure of your firm's own management information systems. Before embarking on an exhaustive collation of relevant data you need to satisfy yourself and principal stakeholders that such information is going to bring a more meaningful conclusion. It must be a questionable exercise if gathering this extra data will incur a significant cost in itself!

At a strategic corporate level the evaluation process is attempting to measure the change from your original starting point towards your goals. In effect you are attempting to say,

> The delegates started at this level and as a result of training they are now at this level; *and* this new level enables them to be more effective at their work.

This in turn will have (x) benefits which are worth (y) to the organization.

Oh, and by the way, the value of (y) is less than we paid for the training!

This means that if you are going to keep the cost of your evaluation process in perspective, it is important to prioritize what you measure.

So how do you decide what is a priority? The problem you are attempting to solve will provide a clue to the key players identified in your stakeholder analysis. These major sponsors will have an influence on your evaluation agenda but you have to be aware of the dangers of being too thinly spread. To merely skim the surface will influence few people and runs the risk that your data will be marginalized. Perhaps not exactly the kiss of death if your project was a one-off, but it could be pretty terminal if you are looking for repeat or further business. Your decisions should be influenced by:

❑ The organizational importance of the training outcomes – don't lose sight of the hand that feeds you.

❑ The volume of training – if many people will be trained over a number of events.

❑ The relative cost of the evaluation process to the cost of the training activity.

So, for example, take a training course designed to enable check-out staff in a supermarket to use a bar-code scanner and integrated weighing system. The desired outcomes might include:

For the organizational stakeholders:

❑ reduced errors at checkout leading to cash savings;

❑ improved stock control – leading to just-in-time ordering;

❑ demonstrate commitment to new technology to competitors.

For managerial stakeholders:

❑ greater flexibility within the work force;

❑ improved customer relations/loyalty due to greater accuracy in charging for goods;

❑ reduced customer waiting time.

For individual staff stakeholders:

❑ improved job satisfaction;

❑ higher level of transferable skills;

❑ less pressure on key-pad skills.

You could look to evaluate all these outcomes but by thinking 'shoestring' you will concentrate on those that are most important to your key players first. So perhaps you would attempt to measure change in areas such as:

❑ reducing cash errors;

❑ the number of customers served per hour;

❑ discovering how many customers are likely to return to your stores;

❑ testing staff morale.

These have been picked for the sake of making a point but you might chose others depending on circumstances.

Hard data could be available in the level of errors (in terms of the number of occurrences and costs) that occur in till transactions and measuring the number of customers passing through the store. Soft data such as customer satisfaction and staff morale would need to be gathered by some form of market research, staff survey and managerial judgement. Measuring performance in these key areas before and after will start to provide information on key stakeholder requirements.

It should not be forgotten that the shoestring training manager is also a stakeholder in this exercise and will be looking for outcomes related to the effectiveness of the training. These outcomes might include:

❑ Were the learning objectives met?

❑ Has the learning been transferred to the work place?

❑ Was this the most cost effective method of training?

Again this list is not exhaustive and your own agenda will pick out the ones most important to you.

MONITORING PROGRESS – THE TECHNIQUES

So far we have only talked about developing your evaluation strategy in terms of the issues you want to measure. Here and there you will have received warnings about not allowing evaluation costs to spiral out of context with the relative cost of the actual training and desired outcomes. But how can you get a grip on the costs without knowing the evaluation techniques that are available and what they might cost?

	Ease of design	Ease of production	Cost of data processing	Stability of hard data	Stability of soft data
Observation	~~~~~~~	~~~~~~	~~~~~~ (manual recording) ~~~ (video recording)	~~~~~~~~	~~~~~
Knowledge tests	~~~~~	~~~~~~~~	~~~~~	~~~~~~~~	~~~~~
Interpersonal skills & attitude tests	~~~	~~~~~~~	~~~	~~~	~~~~~
Psychological tests	~~	~~	~~	~~~~~~~ (ability tests)	~~~~~ (aptitude tests) ~~~ (personality tests)
Unstructured interviews	~~~~~~~	~~~	~~~~~~~~~~	~~~	~~~~~~~
Structured interviews	~~~	~~~~~~~	~~~	~~~~~	~~~~~
Semi-structured interviews	~~~~~	~~~~~	~~~~~	~~~	~~~~~
Questionnaires – structured	~~~	~~~~~	~~	~~~~~	~~
Questionnaires – unstructured	~~~	~~~~~~~~~~	~~~~~~~	~~~	~~~~~
Action plans	~~~~~~~~~~	~~~~~~~~~~	~~	~~	~~
Learning logs	~~~~~	~~~~~~~~	~~~	~~	~~

Figure 6 Comparative analysis of research techniques.

Key: the longer the shoestring the higher the ease/cost/stability
ie. ~ = low ease/cost/stability; ~~~~~~~~~~ = high ease/cost/stability

Evaluation is in essence no different from the advertisements that show before and after pictures. By taking a snap shot before you start, and others during and at the end, you will be able to demonstrate to stakeholders any changes. Using our snap shot analogy, soft data provides the tone and shading to the hard data picture. Taking the camera analogy further, your snapshots can be taken with a variety of lenses, film speeds and lights. It's worth mentioning that keeping your stakeholders in the dark will only work if you have a very sophisticated touch!

There are a number of techniques used in evaluation; we high-light the key ones here and further details are available in Appendix 4.

TECHNIQUES PURPOSE

Observation

a) Content analysis   To look for evidence of learning and transfer of learning to the workplace. Aim of the observation is to:

❏ show whether or not staff can now perform new procedures; and

❏ demonstrate the degree of change that has taken place.

b) Behaviour analysis   Similar to content analysis but focuses on interpersonal skills. Behaviour which is helpful or a hindrance is logged. A matrix is normally used (see Figure 8) to gather the data against the behaviours.

Test/exams   A traditional method of assessment which is often used in written form to test levels of knowledge and understanding, eg open questions, limited answers, multiple choice and in-tray exercises.

	Item/time period						
Controls speed of inward conveyor belt?							
Offers bar code to scanner							
Waits for acceptance tone before releasing item to outward conveyor belt?							
If no acceptance tone, enters cost manually?							
If a warning tone, enters price details as required?							
Weighs fresh produce and waits for acceptance tone?							
etc...							

Figure 7 Content analysis observation sheet.

Key: ✓ = completed correctly,
     ✗ = not completed,
     # = corrected own error.

Negotiation course/meeting held on				(Date)		(Time)		
Participants	Sarah	Brian	Jagdish	John	Nasreen	Paul	Jenny	TOTAL
Interrupting	✓✓✓							
Point scoring	✓	✓✓				✓		
Blaming		✓				✓✓		
Threatening		✓						
Sarcasm								
Listening			✓		✓✓✓		✓✓	
Seeking clarification			✓			✓✓		
Asks open questions	✓			✓✓✓				
Advancing ideas						✓		
(…other behaviours can be used)								
TOTAL								

Shaded behaviours are considered unhelpful in reaching a win-win result.
Adapted from *Behaviour Analysis in Training* by Neil Rackham and Terry Morgan (McGraw-Hill 1977).

Figure 8 Observation sheet for behaviour analysis.

Interpersonal skills and attitude tests

Participants are asked to rate how highly they agree or disagree with given statements. Using behaviour rating scales they are given a series of statements and asked to rate them according to their viewpoint.

Psychological tests

Standard forms of assessment on a range of topics, normally purchased and administered by recognized and qualified practitioners, eg

1. Achievement tests which measure what participants have learned.

2. Ability/aptitude tests attempt to show whether participants could undertake a particular task.

3. Personality/attitude tests show whether participants have the inclination to undertake a task.

Interviews

Interviewing is the traditional information gathering tool. There are basically three types of interview:

1. Unstructured or open interview – free flowing within a range of research.

2. Structured interviews – following a predetermined path.

3. Semi-structured – a mixture of open and structured interviews.

Ten tips for shoestring interviewers

1. Before embarking on a series of interviews ask yourself: Is this the best method for obtaining this information, could I get it some other way more cost effectively?

2. Decide on method and whether individual, group or telephone.

3. Be clear about what you want to know. Categorize your questions under must; should; could ask.

4. Test your questions, watch out for bias.

5. Decide how to record the information from the interview: ie your notes; note-taker or tape recorded – if the last two get the interviewees' permission.

6. When setting up the interview be clear about how long it will last and what it is about.

7. When conducting the interview do not be tempted to deviate from your plan *unless* you can justify it in terms of the quality or importance of the information you are obtaining.

8. Some interviewees think that because they have told you something you will take action on it. Make no promises and don't give the impression you will unless it is in your power to do so. Remember you are there as an interviewer first and trouble-shooter second.

9. Consolidate your notes as soon after the interview as possible. What seemed perfectly clear ten minutes ago can be less so five days later!

10. It pays to be polite and courteous to your informant. They are probably having to give up their time to see you, and you may need to see them again!

Questionnaires   The next best method to interviewing. The approach and planning for a questionnaire is similar to an interview requiring:

❑ clarity about what is being measured;

❑ precision in the wording of questions;

❑ avoid making assumptions about the likely respondent;

❑ keep questions short using simple and straightforward words;

❑ avoid closed and leading questions;

❑ make sure instructions for completion are clear.

Ten tips for producing shoestring questionnaires

1. Is the question essential?

2. Have you considered how you will process this information when it comes back?

3. Can the question be understood? Is there any chance of the object of the question being lost?

4. Will the participants understand what you are talking about? Have you made an unexplained assumption about them?

5. Have you used simple language avoiding jargon?

6. Is the appearance of the questionnaire likely to attract someone to complete it?

7. Is the sequence of questions logical and does it avoid leading the participant?

8. Have you tested or piloted your questionnaire?

9. How will the participants get the completed forms back to you?

10. How will you handle questionnaires not returned, questions unanswered or incomplete answers? How will you cope with the bias effect this may have on the overall results?

	Interviews	Questionnaires
Cost of production	Questions do not necessarily need to be produced in advance, presentation not therefore important.	Good presentation is vital and requires design and preparation considerations. More expensive than interviewing.
Number who can be reached	Limited.	Far-reaching.
Cost of administering	Requires interviewers to cover sample population – additional relative costs includes travel and subsistence.	One person can administer the whole sample population – additional relative costs restricted to printing and postal charges (out and back).
Skills required	Extensive oral skills, limited written skills.	Extensive written skills, limited oral skills.
Flexibility	High possibility to amend questions *in situ*.	Low possibility to amend questions *in situ* without high costs.
Cost of processing	High (very high when transcribing interviews).	Low to medium costs depending on the number of open questions.
Return/completion Rate	Good.	Potentially poor.

Figure 9   Comparison between using interviews and questionnaires.

Action plans   Normally completed at the end of training events to remind participants what they have learned and to place in context of the workplace. Should contain:

❑ clear statement of what will be done and when;

❑ be achievable and realistic;

❑ provide an indication of the support and help needed to overcome barriers to skill and knowledge transfer.

Learning logs   Designed to encourage participants to record significant learning and development points as they go through a training event.

Sampling

An important part of the evaluation will be the number of people from whom you obtain information. Prioritizing your evaluation targets is one way of focusing the spotlight on what is important. Typically a sample will take into account:

❑ those exposed to the training event;

❑ their line managers;

❑ key stakeholders with an interest in the outcomes.

More is said about sampling techniques in Appendix 4.

Session: *Setting the scene*

What I have learned   [ ]
For further consideration   [ ]
For action   [ ]

Session: *Change framework*

What I have learned   [ ]
For further consideration   [ ]
For action   [ ]

Session: *The role of change agent*

What I have learned   [ ]
For further consideration   [ ]
For action   [ ]

Session: *Team development – developing the team*

What I have learned   [ ]
For further consideration   [ ]
For action   [ ]

Session: *Team development – the role of the team leader*

What I have learned   [ ]
For further consideration   [ ]
For action   [ ]

Figure 10   Example of a Learning log.

Use this log to record any ideas or issues you would want to recall, or action to be taken later. You can add further boxes for other key sessions.

REVIEWING RESULTS – PRESENTING THE DATA

Spending time and money gathering evaluation data is a fairly meaningless exercise unless you do something with it. Evaluation results will need to feed into some kind of action and decision making processes. As you will have seen, evaluation interventions will have been made throughout most of the systematic training cycle. This raises the question of when you should publish the information you have gained. The main driver in answering this question has to be the attitude of your stakeholders. The matrix below might help in that decision of who to tell what and when.

Level of commitment

		LOW	HIGH
Level of power or authority in the organization			
	HIGH	Keep pleased	Keep in the picture (key players)
	LOW	Limited energy!	Keep in touch

During a stakeholder analysis you will have established the varying levels of interest amongst the stakeholders. Major organizational sponsors may be content with agreeing the strategic issues and will only want to see Step 5 (systematic training cycle) data. Line managers of the participants may want to know whether training objectives are being met. Those presenting or facilitating will want to know how effective an individual event or session was. Clarifying these levels of reporting is Step 1.

The style and tone of your report will depend on your organization but the points you will need to get across should include sufficient information to make informed decisions. So for the actual training event issues such as:

❑ Are learning objectives being met?

❑ Have individual learning goals been addressed?

❑ Will learning be transferred back to the workplace?

❑ Have training methods been effective?

will have been a feature.

A key player in the learning and evaluation process is the participants' line manager. These people are in a unique position. They are able to assess the needs beforehand and to judge whether any improvements have taken place, and to quantify how useful that improvement has been in bottom-line terms. In order to help them achieve this role in the evaluation process they should receive information about the training event and be encouraged to brief their member of staff on how this will fit into their work. On the participant's return to the workplace, debriefing should take place with the line manager to help consolidate any plan of action. At regular intervals the line manager can then check on progress. Many organizations already expect their managers to take an active part in the development of their staff. For the shoestring manager evaluating training, this is a excellent occasion to draw further data.

A report on the effectiveness of the training at an organizational level should be answering questions such as:

❑ How far has the training delivered selected outcomes?

❑ Has anything unforeseen been learned?

❑ How much did it cost (in total and by key components)?

❑ Was it worth it?

❑ Could another method have been more cost effective?

Depending on the evaluation methods you have employed you may wish to include some of the collated data and perhaps highlight some individual comments. However, do not swamp your audience with statistics. While you may find them fascinating, your data has to be relevant and support your conclusions. Decisions should flow from the evaluation report – not confusion! To help with the presentation of your evaluation data see the model contents page below.

Framework for presenting evaluation findings

1. Contents.

2. An outline of the purpose of the evaluation including the evaluation criteria.

3. An executive summary (ie a summary of conclusions and recommendations).

4. Main text.
   ❏ summary of background to the training;
   ❏ summary of the scope of the evaluation and the method used;
   ❏ statement of the findings;
   ❏ the implication of the findings;
   ❏ recommendations for action based on findings.

5. Concluding remarks.

6. Appendices:

   ❏ description of the methods used, the sample used, etc;
   ❏ raw data from which conclusions have been drawn; (optional: it can be a distraction from the action needed and can compromise the confidentiality of the individuals);
   ❏ Case studies (if applicable).

A further feature you need to consider is whether to include an assessment of the effectiveness of the evaluation strategy:

   ❏ Has it provided all that was expected of it?
   ❏ Could it have been better focused?
   ❏ Did you allow for the unexpected?
   ❏ What did it cost in percentage terms of the total cost?
   ❏ Would you do it differently next time?

FINAL THOUGHTS ON EVALUATION

In conclusion, remember that although evaluation can be expensive and time consuming, it needn't be so. Not everything needs to be evaluated all the time. Important issues have to be fully examined, particularly where the results have an organizational or bottom line impact. You do not need to be a researcher or statistician to get quality results. Above all keep in mind that the evaluation process needs to start long before the actual training is delivered.

Personal growth

We have spent the majority of this book focusing on skill development and how to operate successfully as a shoestring manager. It is also important to develop a strategy for your own personal development and growth. As a shoestring manager we have acknowledged that you could have a variety of roles, however within those roles you may need to:

- ❏ handle change;
- ❏ manage a higher profile within the business;
- ❏ respond to increased responsibility;
- ❏ handle pressure;
- ❏ operate within different working patterns;
- ❏ resist longer working hours.

Depending on your role you may find that you have to cope with some or all of the above. So how do you deal with the issues that might arise from these situations?

HANDLING CHANGE

What is change? Much has been written about change management and 'change agents'. Change can be interpreted in different ways, but in reality most modern organizations are constantly evolving, and so the shoestring manager has to recognize how this process may impact on their role and their working environment.

In the foreword to this book we highlighted a shoestring manager profile and it is this skill set that will help you to handle change. Later in this chapter we discuss other aspects of that profile, but gaining an understanding of the 'big picture' and identifying the part you play in it is very important whatever your role.

MANAGING A HIGHER PROFILE WITHIN THE BUSINESS

As we stated above, it is unlikely that any organization will stand still and so the shoestring manager needs to develop their own power base and use influencing skills to talk with assurance to senior management. It is important to identify the important people within the organization: who are the decision makers, what impact might they have on your role or your success? What can you do to influence them? How might they fit into your network? Although this may seem to be manipulative, it is more about having control over your own destiny. This has often been a hard lesson for people affected by restructuring or downsizing to discover that the organization for whom they had loyally worked for many years no longer required their services.

Changes in today's working practices is likely to lead to an adoption of a portfolio management approach, when employees manage a range of working contracts; self employment, part-time roles and non-executive responsibilities (see Recommended Reading list for details of *Portfolio Working* by Joanna Grigg, published by Kogan Page).

We have illustrated on a number of occasions throughout this book the importance of linking with the business objectives. Depending on your role the following list will apply to you:

❑ Taking on responsibility for coaching new ways of working into the organization.

❑ Contributing ideas which illustrate how T&D can help to move the business forward.

❑ Demonstrating how the function can be more proactive and involved in the business.

❑ Working in partnership with the business and senior management.

To be able to achieve this you should regularly ask yourself the following questions:

1. Do I understand the overall vision, values and direction of this business?

2. Do I have sufficient business knowledge to be able to work closely with the business?

3. Do I have contact with the right people? Can I influence decisions?

4. What channels of communication can I use?

5. What can I do to market my services?

RESPOND TO INCREASED RESPONSIBILITY

There is every likelihood that the shoestring manager will find themselves with increased responsibility, and as result you need to think very carefully about planning your workload. It will be important to establish where your role fits within the overall business strategy.

You will need to demonstrate through your personal performance the competencies required by the business. Managers at all levels in today's organizations are being encouraged to take more responsibility. Major decisions are debated further down the organization, and effective two-way communication is seen as a key feature in organizational development.

LOOKING AFTER YOURSELF

In our companion book *Everything you Ever Needed to Know About Training* we used a term 'being comfortable with yourself' and it is a principal that we endorse here. We use the phrase to describe the inner confidence that comes from knowing your strengths and areas of development. It is important to ask for and absorb feedback into your ongoing development.

This feedback should also be viewed pragmatically, as we mentioned above, as the better you know yourself the more you are in control of what you want to do in life. When organizations undergo periods of change, roles and responsibilities that you once assumed might have been part of your career path may no longer exist. It is important that you recognize this, but also have the ability to view this information positively and to adjust accordingly.

As a shoestring manager it is likely that your role will be more visible, there may be increased responsibilities and you may find yourself working for longer periods of time. Therefore it is critically important that you take time out to identify ways of looking after yourself.

You may wonder why we wrote *resist* longer working hours above. There is a famous saying that no one on their death bed would say 'I wish I had spent longer in the office' and so despite pressures to work harder, the key is found in another famous phrase 'work smarter, not harder'.

One of the real issues for many employees operating within restricted budgetary circumstances, or following re-engineering or organizational change, is a belief that the key to success is to be seen to work long hours.

Many people are nervous of being the first to leave the staff carpark, and so they may spend time pushing paper around or doing mindless tasks whiling away the minutes until they feel that it is acceptable to leave. What is needed is a mature approach and the development of a style of working which reflects the organizational need, but also helps everyone to achieve a balanced lifestyle.

This is not to ignore the fact that there will be times when you have to work late; it is instead to try and adopt a more realistic approach to working which will help you to withstand the pressures associated with being a shoestring manager.

BEING ORGANIZED

One of the key principles behind this book is the need to look carefully at your role and apply the shoestring approach. As part of this is a recognition that if your role has changed your priorities may also have a different emphasis. One of the challenges facing many people in today's working environment is balancing the pressures of home and work.

Many shoestring managers may find themselves working within a more flexible environment often with periods of time 'hot-desking' or working in the field or at home. You may also find yourself without secretarial backup, and many of today's managers share a 'pool' secretary and are expected to type their own letters on their personal computer.

Against this background, being organized is immensely important. T&D generates an enormous amount of paperwork: flipcharts, training manuals, catalogues, details of courses, evaluations, etc. If you do not have a permanent base what do you do?

First, identify with your organization what is available, and then think creatively about what needs to be kept as part of your recording system, what could be kept by the training providers, or the individual participants themselves. A question you must always pose yourself when you see paperwork advancing in your direction is 'Do I really need a copy of this?'

There are numerous books on the market about time management and personal organization and we list several in the Recommended Reading list, and although it requires a certain amount of personal sacrifice in the early stages to set systems up, there really is a payback later when you have your systems up and running.

It is also important to recognize that it is often not just time management that is important, but also priority management, particularly when you are working with a number of business functions. We discussed this in Chapter 2 when we took you through the process of prioritizing training needs. It can however be more of a challenge to prioritize our own personal ways of working to provide us with a balanced lifestyle.

Shoestring checklist – priority management

✓ There is only so much time.

✓ Think creatively about the situation.

✓ Identify key activities for the week ahead.

✓ Recognize units of time.

✓ Set up your diary with key meetings and weekly actions.

✓ Identify your priorities for the day.

✓ Respond positively to others people's requests.

✓ Allow time for other people's priorities to enter your list.

✓ Check, review and amend each day.

✓ Identify pressure points and set plan to cope with them.

✓ Have a set of strategies for handling stress and re-energizing.

✓ Work towards a set of focused outcomes and review progress.

HANDLING PRESSURE

There are a number of studies that have been written about the difference between stress and pressure (see Recommended Reading list). We can handle a considerable amount of pressure, but when we become overloaded with a number of difficult situations we may find ourselves exhibiting the symptoms of stress.

The shoestring manager needs to develop strategies for handling pressure and develop a pattern of working which helps him to re-energize and prepare for the potentially difficult periods of work. This could include planning regular breaks: one of the outcomes of reduced resources is sometimes the misguided belief that it could be unwise to go away on holiday because the business might change again while you are away!

In reality most businesses have to withstand long periods of change and transition, and so encouraging employees to go on holiday will have little impact on the overall stability of the business. In fact it will more likely act to improve business because people will be less tired and hopefully will return refreshed. What can have a positive effect is planning your holidays so that you get more regular breaks rather than taking one long break in the summer.

When people are working under periods of pressure there is often a tendency to either go home and crash out in front of the television or to go on somewhere with colleagues from the office, start drinking, and then go home to bed. Ideally you should try to vary the activities to include a mixture of social events which are unrelated to work, as well as taking part in some kind of physical activities during the week to help you build up your stamina. It is also important to study your patterns of eating and to plan a diet which suits your lifestyle.

It is also important to build in some special events and have a good support network, both in and outside work. Everyone should have a mentor, even in a shoestring organization. It may not be part of a formal mentoring process, but identifying someone who understands your situation and who will regularly act as a sounding board for you is critical whatever role you perform.

PERSONAL DEVELOPMENT PLANS

We discussed Personal Development Plans in Chapter 5, but as well as using them as a tool to develop others you should also develop your own plans. Traditionally PDPs have been viewed as primarily focused on the workplace, but organizations are recognizing the importance of providing a balance between workstyle and lifestyle to achieve satisfaction from the combination of work and external activities, which may be involvement in community activities, sport and leisure, or further education.

At the start of each year the people in control of their own lives will sit down and identify their overall goals for the year, which will normally be a mixture of work and personal objectives. These will be recorded and reviewed at regular intervals during the year, and during this process may be modified or added to as the circumstances change. This process is personal to the individual, but logically the work-related goals could be underpinned by personal development plans which they may review with their manager.

Although we can only briefly consider this aspect here, it is a fundamental aspect of any career development plan. You should ask yourself the following questions:

1. What are my overall goals for the next twelve months?

2. What specific objectives do I have?

3. How can I meet these objectives?

4. What activities do I need to plan into my work?

5. Is this current role leading anywhere?

6. How can I benefit from the experiences in this role?

7. How can I extend this role to gain a broader understanding of this business?

8. What further training and development do I need?

9. Would secondment be possible? Why would it help me?

10. What networking opportunities do I have?

11. How could I raise my profile?

12. Where do I want to be in twelve months?

These are just a sample of the types of questions you can ask yourself. Employers are no longer impressed that you have achieved an MBA or other further qualification, they also want to know how you are using it. It is also worth noting that this approach is not something that you just do at the start of your career; it can help you positively handle change throughout your life as you move from job to job, through periods of unemployment, self employment and into retirement.

Adopting a proactive approach to your own development is not only important in a personal sense, but it also means that you will have a better understanding of how to help other people manage their own careers. In today's working environment everyone needs an up-to-date and upbeat CV, which clearly demonstrates how you are managing your career and using any qualifications that you might have achieved.

And finally...

The training on a shoestring
Top 10

1. Adopt a value for money *not* the cheapest price philosophy. X

2. Build relationships with the business, suppliers and training X colleagues in other businesses.

3. Adopt a co-ordinations overview to the delivery of training and learning solutions.

4. Explore a wide variety of funding solutions.

5. Take account of different learning styles. X

6. Identify with senior management the overall mission, vision, values and business objectives.

7. Explore the full range of learning solutions. X

8. Be selective in your use of external resources. X

9. Remember not to neglect your own personal development.

10. Always think SHOESTRING before undertaking any major investment.

We hope you enjoyed reading this book... let us know your shoestring solutions!

Appendix 1:
Stakeholder analysis:
influence grid

Stakeholders	Their role	Significance in gaining commitment High/medium/low	Action to take
Depot supervisors	Managers of trainees	High	Involvement in training needs analysis; Keep them in touch with development; Secure release of trainees; Make sure training worked (ie get feedback on training).
Depot handlers	Potential delegates	High	Involvement in training needs analysis; Let them know its going to happen and when; Make sure the training is working.
Managing Director	Head of company	Low	Make sure s\he knows the training is being arranged.
Rigsby & Co.	Key customers	Medium	We need to know if closing the depot for training will cause them a problem. Could help with training needs analysis.
... etc			

Appendix 2:
Proforma for initially assessing resources available and required

Issue	What & where available?	Required?	Acquired?
Money			
Deadlines – time available			
Participants' time in salary and expenses costs			
Trainers' salaries and expenses			
Accommodation including offices and training rooms			
Office equipment (computers, photocopiers, etc)			
Training equipment (OHPs, flip charts, etc)			
Production and printing of training material			
Stationery and other consumables			
… include any others			

Appendix 3: Problem work sheet

A clear statement of the problem (in terms of outcomes rather than a strategy):
Solutions considered:
Additional solutions generated by the set:
Planned course of action (expressed in terms of desired outcomes, tasks to be completed and measurable standards):
Report of action taken including successes and areas for further action/problem solving:

Appendix 4:
Evaluation techniques

OBSERVATION

This technique can be used both during and after the training event to look for evidence of learning and transfer of that learning to the workplace. If used in a structured way it provides a reasonable level of objectivity. The more unstructured the observation the higher the risk of subjectivity creeping into your data.

During a course observation can be used to check that a participant was completing tasks correctly using these simple steps:

1. Establish before the training event the various actions they need to do and the manner in which they have to be performed.

2. Observation during the training establishes whether they are following the correct procedure.

3. By feeding this information back they can improve their performance before taking up the task for real on the shop floor.

This is sometimes referred to as content analysis/observation; an example of an analysis sheet is in Chapter 7, Figure 7.

The aim of such observation is to: (a) show whether or not staff can now perform new procedures; and (b) demonstrate the degree of change that has taken place.

Measuring the degree of change becomes more significant when participants already have an existing level of expertise and may have experienced a truncated version of the training. In these situations it may be necessary to perform some kind of pretraining snapshot to feed into any cost effectiveness calculations. This consideration is a general one which you will need to consider for most training strategies.

For measuring interpersonal skills a similar technique called behaviour analysis is used. When using this technique we log the actual behaviours that are helpful or a hindrance to achieving the desired outcomes. The steps are the same as for content analysis but a matrix similar to that in Figure 7, would be used to gather the data. The categories of behaviour would alter depending on the skills involved.

Observational evaluation can be also used in the workplace to test whether the training is being put into practice. A useful aid in this technique is video although this normally increases the time need to process the data. When reporting to stakeholders you are aiming to make links between the original desired outcomes, the training provided, and the actions demonstrated in a 'live' environment.

TESTS/EXAMS

A traditional method of assessment which is often used in written forms more for testing levels of knowledge and understanding than interpersonal skills. When used before or at the start of the training event, this method can provide a benchmark. Later testing using similar instruments can demonstrate levels of improvement (or otherwise). Practical tests depend heavily on the skill of the examiner to spot the desired features.

Knowledge tests include:

Open questions: essay-type responses required;

Limited answers: participants are asked to complete a sentence or phrase;

Multiple choice: participants are given a choice of two (ie yes/no or true/false) or more possible answers to choose from;

In-tray exercise: participants are expected to work their way through a typical days work interacting where necessary with the examiners.

Interpersonal skills and attitude tests

Participants are asked to rate how highly they agree or disagree with given statements, eg:
'Do you…
a) strongly disagree
b) agree more than disagree

c) are uncertain
d) disagree more than agree
e) strongly agree.

… with the statements' eg
'I think it is better to act than do nothing.'
'I prefer to do things myself rather than delegate.'

Behaviour rating scales – given a series of statements about behaviours, say as a manager, participants rate their skills on a scale of 1 to 10 (low to high).

Psychological tests

These are standard forms of assessment on a range of topics which can be purchased. They generally fall into three categories, with diminishing reliability the higher the level:

Achievement test (Level 1) – shows what participants have learned or say they have learned and are fairly conclusive.

Ability/aptitude test (Level 2) – endeavours to show whether participants could undertake a particular task if asked to, and gives good indication as to intellectual capability.

Personality/attitude test (Level 3) – attempts to show whether participants have the inclination to undertake a task can only provide a likely indication.

Although it is possible to purchase sets of these tests, suppliers usually insist that they are administered by suitably qualified practitioners.

Any instrument that uses participants' views of themselves needs to carry a health warning. The views they have of themselves do not always match the perspective of those around them !

INTERVIEWS

Interviewing is the traditional information-gathering tool of the researcher, which enables the interviewer to explore a variety of situations such as:

❑ assessing people, perhaps for a job;

❑ gathering data for a study or evaluation;

❑ testing and sounding out ideas;

❑ obtaining peoples' opinions, such as in market research.

A skilful interviewer gathers information effectively by encouraging the informant; formulating and asking focused questions while displaying appropriate non-verbal behaviour. Interviewing is a skill and there are no set rules to follow to guarantee a particular result. This is one of the weaknesses and strengths of employing interviewing as an evaluation technique.

Turning to question techniques, there are basically three types of interview:

1. Unstructured or open – the interview is free-ranging although within the boundaries of your research.

2. Structured – the interview follows a present path.

3. Semi-structured – a mixture of the other two interviewing approaches.

Each method can be very effective depending on the results you are seeking and how much time and money you have got at your disposal.

Unstructured interviews

Conducting an unstructured interview is akin to trawling for fish. You cast your net over the side and when it is pulled back on board you have a collection of different fish. Some are very interesting but others are not what you are seeking and get thrown back. Occasionally you will even come across a real gem but there is no guarantee that you will get one every time. If you do not use care in choosing the fishing area you could end up with a net full of useless junk!

The object of the unstructured interview is to discover a person or group of peoples' ideas and opinions about a given topic. Although the interview is unstructured in terms of prepared questions you will be looking to seek views on a range of issues within your topics area. Unlike a social conversation the interview will be within a context, either of training need or training evaluation. This technique allows you to explore what are the important issues and has no preconceived ideas of where the answers lie.

In order to stay within the topics area it is sometimes useful to have a framework of the critical suggest factors you are hoping to investigate with possible associated 'starter' questions. This will not only allow you to stay within the evaluation subject but can provide a stimulus should the interview start to dry up. So if, for example, you were attempting to evaluate project management training your key topics might be:

❑ Quality of report writing (what differences have you noticed in your staff's reports)?

❑ The costing of projects (how would you rate your group's ability to estimate costs)?

❑ Management of projects (what sort of unforseen problems do your projects have)?

❑ Team working (tell me about team spirit).

From the information given, you are looking for clues around which to formulate other areas for investigation. The freedom of the unstructured interview allow you to explore issues as they arise, following the direction and logic of the interviewee. Although this freedom enables new perspectives to be examined, keeping a note of what is said can be very difficult. To overcome this you can either:

❑ Take brief notes during the interview, although this may inhibit your ability to follow what is being said.

❑ Get someone else to take notes on your behalf, although their presence may inhibit the interviewee.

❑ Tape record the interview, although as well as being an inhibiting factor it can take quite some time to transcribe accurately.

❑ Use none of the above but write up as full an account as you can recall immediately after the interview.

All of these have their advantages and disadvantages which need to be assessed against the level of importance of the information gained and the cost of collecting. The shoestring manager needs to assess that level of importance alongside the relative importance of the stakeholder being interviewed. The Director of Corporate Operations might be a touch more important to record fully than a client who has only used your organization once or twice – but only you will know!

The advantage of the unstructured interview is that you could conduct a few in-depth interviews in order to identify and then formulate more structured interviews with a wider audience. The down side of unstructured interviews is that the quality of the information does depend heavily on the skills of the interviewer to get people to talk about the issues. The interviews and the data-sifting afterwards can be very time consuming. If can be so frustrating to have conducted a two hour interview to find at the end you have learned very little. Sometimes an insight can be very revealing but as the fairytale princess said on finding her prince, 'you have to kiss a heck of a lot of frogs first!'

Structured interviews

Structured interviews are designed to obtain information by using a set of standard questions which can be framed in one of three ways:

1. Open-ended (eg what other topics do you think the training should have covered?).

2. Closed (eg did you know how to clear a paper jam – yes/no).

3. Scale rating (eg how often do you use this technique in your normal work – a lot/some/not at all?).

This type of interview:

❑ Provides a degree of consistency when interviewing a number of respondents.

❑ Offers a degree of control over the amount of time each interview takes.

❑ Allows direct comparison with answers to similar questions.

❑ Makes the analysis of the data more manageable.

❑ Provides a structure for inexperienced interviewers.

Although this technique limits scope for going outside set questions; for the shoestring manager with little time or experience in these matters such an approach is highly attractive.

More is said in the section dealing with questionnaires about question construction, but you should always categorize your interview questions into those which you

MUST (high priority)

SHOULD (medium priority)

COULD (lowest priority) ask.

Semi-structured interviews

When constructing the question set it is sometimes necessary to ask a combination of the three types of question. Although from a collation perspective it may be useful to able to say that 75 per cent of the target population could clear a paper jam, your stakeholder may also want to know why 25 per cent could not. A fixed or scale rating question can be followed by an open question such as 'why do you give it that rating?' This approach of allowing more open-ended responses to effectively a closed question is referred to as semi-structured. While it is tempting to open up an interview to such further exploration, you should always bear in mind the purpose of the information gathered and whether you will have the capacity to process the data.

Although most of the examples of interviewing whether unstructured or structured have concentrated on talking to individuals it is sometime useful to interview groups of people. Although these are more demanding to facilitate, the interaction between colleagues who have worked or studied together can reveal a deeper level of information. Given usual group dynamics you are less likely to obtain personal information. If you are facilitating a group it is usually helpful to have someone else acting as note taker.

If you are short of time a variation on the face-to-face interview is one via a telephone. Provided the person you are calling is aware of your intentions and can spare the time, telephone interviewing can enable you to speak to people over a wide geographical area without the need to spend time on travel. It is just the job for the shoestring manager working in a company spread all over the country. Sometimes it is desirable to give some warning of the issue you wish to explore so that the interviewee can gather their thoughts and papers as necessary. Having booked the time and date when you will call, you could let the people have a copy of your framework of issues or a copy of the questions. In that way they will be more focused. It helps overcome the lack of non-verbal communication although your tone of voice will play a large part in these interviews.

Before embarking on a series of interviews there are one or two health warnings the shoestring manager needs to be aware of. First, interviews can take up more time that you allow for especially if you come across someone who does not have the same time constraints as you. At the other end of this spectrum is the interviewee who is not prepared to give you all the time you need to conduct the interview. The answer to both situations is discipline. In the first case you must set a time for the interview to last and stick to it. This is only courteous to the person you are seeing. Having categorized your information needs and sticking to them, you are less likely to be the wrong side of a door saying, 'If only'! Figure 9 in Chapter 7, page 98 provides a checklist when considering interviews.

QUESTIONNAIRES

Although interviewing participants and other stakeholders may seem the most attractive way to obtain evaluation data, it is not always the most practical in terms of the time you have to spend getting to and conducting the interview and then processing the data. Not forgetting, of course, the cost of everyones' salaries. If you cannot get there in person, often the next best method is to send a questionnaire as you will be reducing some of the expense, an essential for the shoestring manager. To a certain extent, closed and scale-rating interview questions are almost face-to-face administered questionnaires.

From the outset it has to be recognized that designing effective questionnaires is a demanding task. It is not a case of simply jotting down a series of questions and printing them off in a form. With the interview you always have the option of adjusting a question that does not seem to hit the target, but with a questionnaire often the person completing the form is some distance from the author. It can be soul destroying to send out a batch of questionnaires only to see from those that do get returned that the respondents have missed the point you were seeking to address. If the questionnaire is really poor it will probably end up in the bin after the first few questions have been read. It helps to remember that the questionnaire is a tool of measurement, in this case measuring change brought about by training. It could equally be about measuring the gap between present levels and a desired level of skill and knowledge as used in training needs analysis.

The approach and planning for a questionnaire is no different to that of an interview. You need to be clear what it is you are trying to measure. What are the essential, key elements that you need to know about? These will have their roots in the early data collection you did with your stakeholders. They should be categorized in the same way as interview outcomes,

MUST (high priority)

SHOULD (medium priority)

COULD (lowest priority) ask.

Having placed your topics into an order of priority, start putting into words the questions that will give you, when answered, this data. A preliminary consideration is the composition of your intended target population. Each question needs to be formulated in such a way as to ensure it is :

❑ *Clear* what you are asking; avoid using words and jargon that the participants will not understand, otherwise your question could miss the mark and leave you with information that at best is ambiguous or worse is misleading.

❑ Worded in a *precise* way; without precision there is a danger that your question will tap into unrelated data. The information could be very interesting but may have strayed from an aim to measure the effect of your training.

❑ Free of any *assumptions* about the likely respondent; a question like, ' Do your staff have a computer,' makes the assumption that participants have staff. Even if they do, it is not clear whether if it is their personal property or a company computer.

If overcoming such pitfalls proves difficult try providing explanatory notes to help guide people. Be aware that this runs the risk of introducing a bias and could make the questionnaire overlong. There is a checklist on page 97 in Chapter 7 to assist with the formulation of questionnaires.

The presentation of the questionnaire is vital if someone is going to give it any quality time. In the same way that you may receive rejections from stakeholders you wish to interview, it is even easier to reject a questionnaire. Here are a few ground rules to help reduce the risk of instant rejection:

❑ keep the questions short;

❑ avoid double-barrelled questions;

❑ avoid double negatives;

❑ use simple and straight forward words;

❑ do not use closed questions unless following an open question;

❑ avoid leading questions;

❑ steer away from sensitive questions;

❑ Use plenty of space on the form, do not overcrowd the page;

❑ make sure instructions are clear, ie how many boxes should they tick;

❑ allow yourself space on the form to process the data.

In addition to using text questions you could use some of the techniques mentioned in earlier sections such as interpersonal skills, attitude or achievement tests. An alternative, but perhaps expensive, approach could be to provide video, audio or computer material and ask the participant to answer related questions.

If you have some doubt whether to use either interviewing or questionnaire techniques, Figure 9 in Chapter 7, page 98 has a brief comparison of the main advantages and disadvantages of both approaches.

ACTION PLANS

Action plans can be completed at the end of training events as a form of reminder to participants about what they have learned and to place that in the context of their workplace. Although strictly speaking part of the transfer of learning, action plans can provide a very useful source of evaluation data. However to do so they need to:

❑ contain a clear statement of what will be done and when;

❑ be achievable and realistic; and

❑ provide an indication of support and help needed to overcome barriers to skill and knowledge transfer.

By analysing action plans and later actual achievements it is possible to measure change in a quantifiable way. Provided the action undertaken is within the context of the training events objects, this method can provide a rich vein of information.

LEARNING LOGS

By encouraging participants to record their more significant learning or development points as they go through a training event, these can also be a valuable source of evaluation data for later action. An example of such a log for a management of change course, can be found in Figure 10 in Chapter 7, pages 100–19.

This method can reveal a range of information about the effectiveness of the training methods and how the participant plans to transfer the learning back. In the example given, the additional development dimension could provide a clue as to future training needs. Although structured around each session this type of questionnaire is unstructured and therefore can result in data processing problems.

SAMPLING

When considering your evaluation strategy an important component will be the number of people from whom you obtain information. If time and resources were not a problem you could include everyone involved for every training event you organized. In reality few organizations can operate such a blank-cheque policy. Those that could, would not do so as such an approach would not provide value for money.

Prioritizing your evaluation targets is one way of focusing the spotlight on what is important. Sampling is one technique to help provide a value for money focus by selecting a suitable group from which to obtain data. Your approach to sampling will depend on the importance of the measurement you are trying to achieve.

Complex sampling processes will normally only appeal to the shoestring manager when the outcomes are highly significant to the core existence of an organization. In most situations a lesser commitment to such absolute values will be acceptable.

The basic sampling principle is the probability that a smaller group can have the same attributes/characteristics as the total stakeholder population. This is sometimes referred to as 'probability sampling'. In order for this smaller group to be regarded as representative it will need to offer the same variables you wish to evaluate. This will depend on the outcomes you are attempting to measure, but typically a sample will take into account issues such as:

❑ those exposed to the training event;

❑ their line managers;

❑ (key) stakeholders with an interest or affected by the outcomes.

Who to include depends on what you want to know, how you will process the information and what the evaluation will cost in total. To obtain immediate reaction sheets at the end of a course may be relatively cheap if the participants' time is already spoken for as part of the course. You are likely to get a 100 per cent return, particularly if you stand by the door before they can get out! However, the quality of this information may be subject to the participants willingness to give considered answers in the time available before they leave the course. So called 'happiness sheets' are notorious in providing a euphoric picture which is not necessarily sustained when the participants have to apply what they have learned in the workplace.

Taking up line manager and other key stakeholders' time, in effect taking them away from their immediate core business, is another matter. The size of the sample is not everything but targeting is. A properly devised evaluation sample can give far more reliable data than a scattergun approach. At the end of the day your sample will probably be constrained by the time and the cost of administration and analysis.

Remember the actual sample may be different from those who actually reply. Part of your evaluation strategy must be able to cope with people who do not reply or give incomplete answers. The credibility of your data is important and should avoid the risk of being discredited due to bias or weaknesses in your sampling tactics. You need to be more interested in obtaining tenable information which is easily accessible at a moderate cost rather than in-depth data gathered at high cost.

How to avoid bias? The sample and the questions asked should not be designed to influence the likely answers. To avoid sampling bias try to ensure your sample is more or less representative to all people you could have included in the sample. For example, if 35 per cent of the participants are managers and 65 per cent are shop assistants your sample should mirror this ratio.

The risk of including unwittingly biased questions can be reduced by testing your evaluation techniques out in a small pilot exercise. Testers would be asked for their views on issues such as the ease of completion, bias and feasibility to outcomes being measured. If the issue of bias is an important one to overcome, a second or even third person could be asked to put the questions to see if there are different responses from the same person. Complete objectivity is what you will be seeking to achieve.

The shoestring manager should ask for vital information. Use the discipline of, 'If I could only get, say, five pieces of information, what would they be?' When designing questionnaires it can be very tempting to be self indulgent and to lose sight of your goals. Ask yourself 'Would I answer this if it was sent to me?' Remain disciplined; or run the risk of getting nothing back!

Appendix 5:
Personal Development Plan

Description of Current Role, what is working well, what needs to be developed or improved.
Description of new skills or knowledge that I need to gain.
Method of achieving the above. Target Date:
Longer term goals or aspirations. Target Date:

Name:	Name of Manager:
Signature:	Signature:
Date:	Date:

Recommended reading

Belasco, James A (1990) *Teaching the Elephant to Dance: Empowering Change in your Organisation* Hutchinson Business, London.

Belbin, Meredith B. (1981) *Management Teams* Heinemann, London.

Black, Jack (1994) *Mindstore* Thorsons, London.

Boydell, Tom (1983) *A Guide to the Identification of Training Needs* BACIE, London.

Bramley, Peter (1986) *Evaluation of Training, A Practical Guide* BACIE, London.

Brown, Mark (1993) *The Dinosaur Strain* Innovation Centre Europe Ltd.

Buzan, Tony *Use Your Head* (4th edn 1995) BBC, London.

Buzan, Tony, and Buzan, Barry (1993) *The Mind Map Book* BBC, London.

Cohen, Louis and Manion, Lawrence (1989) *Research Methods in Education* Routledge, London.

Grigg, Joanna (1997) *Portfolio Working: A practical guide to thriving in a changing workplace* Kogan Page, London.

Hammer, Michael and Champy, James (1993) *Re-engineering the Corporation* Harper Collins, USA and (1993) Nicholas Brealey, London.

Handy, Charles (1994) *The Empty Raincoat* Hutchinson, London.

Honey, Peter, and Mumford, Alan (1982) *Manual of Learning Styles* Honey, Maidenhead.

Jeffers, Susan (1987) *Feel the Fear and do it anyway* Century Hutchinson, London.

Josephs, Ray, (1994 revised edn) *How to gain an extra hour every day* Thorsons, London.

Kanter, Rosabeth M (1983) *The Change Masters* Allen & Unwin, London.

Kanter, Rosabeth M (1989) *When Giants Learn to Dance* Simon & Schuster, London.

Kolb, David A, Rubin, I M and McIntyre, J M (4th edn 1994) *Organisational Psychology, an experiential approach to organisational behavior* Prentice-Hall, London.

Malone, Samuel A (1997) *How to set up and Manage a Corporate Learning Centre* Gower, Aldershot

McNally, David (1993) *Even Eagles Need a Push* Thorsons, London.

O'Connor, Joseph and Seymour, John (1990) *Introducing NLP Neuro Linguistic Programming* Mandala, London.

O'Connor, Joseph and Seymour, John (1994) *Training with NLP, Skills for Managers, Trainers and Communicators* Thorsons, London.

Oppenheim, AN (1992) *Questionnaire Design, Interviewing and Attitude Measurement* Pinter Publishers, London.

Pedler, Mike (ed.) (1991) *Action Learning in Practice* (2nd edn) Gower, Aldershot.

Peters, Tom (1992) *Liberation Management* Macmillan, London.

Peters, Tom, and Austin, Nancy (1985) *A Passion for Excellence* Collins, London.

Revans, RW (1982) *The Origins and Growth of Learning* Chartwell Bratt, Bromley.

Scott, Amanda, (1997) *Learning Centres, A Step-by-Step Guide to*

Planning , Managing and Evaluating an Organizational Resource Centre Kogan Page, London.

Thorne, Kaye and Mackey, David, *Everything you Ever Needed to Know About Training* (1996) Kogan Page, London.

Index